PILLBOXES

A Study of UK Defences 1940

PILLBOXES

A Study of UK Defences 1940

Henry Wills

LEO COOPER
in association with
SECKER AND WARBURG

CONTENTS

ACKNOWLEDGEMENTS

With well over 1,000 people helping in this nationwide survey, I thank each one for their help, whether they sent a single site or a list of dozens. There were those who did more and supplied drawings, photographs and other information, enough to fill this book. Some are mentioned in the text, but my special thanks go to; David Barnes, Hugh Cave, Peter Cobb of United Kingdom Fortifications Club, Peter Connon, John Gamblin, Terry Gander, John Gerken, Brig J. R. E. Hamilton Baillie, Mrs O. Hasson, Michael Hodges, D. E. Hutt, Anthony Kemp, Murray Maclean, W. E. Parker, Michael Payne, A. C. Pinhorn, R. R. P. Rogers, Peter Sly, Victor Smith, L. A. Thomas, Lt-Col A. F. Toogood, Paul Tritton, Capt A. B. Sainsbury, John Kenyon, Charles Trollope, A. Fenwick, Tom Dewar, Mark Elsen, Henry Manning, Dr C. M. Dring, G. W. Harrington, K. H. Walpole, Andrew Selkirk, Lesley Grant-Adamson, Pat Bromley, Ron Pickersgill, The Tyrrells County Primary School at Chelmsford, P. W. B. Semmens, Michael Wheeler, J. N. Pace, Miss P. R. Miller, David Newbold, J. R. Marshall, David Barton, Tony Fishlock, Duncan Godwin, Winston Ramsey, Nigel Ruckley, Philip Kenton, David Leslie, John Cross, E. Varty, Dennis Sloper, Christopher Hall, Dr Gerry Tidy, G. M. Tuke, Robert Kinzie, George Rochester, Maj Harry King, Margaret Pinsent, Ted Hooton, Ian Goodger, Doug Ball, W. R. M. Maxwell and Ray Selkirk. My apologies to those who I've missed.

In addition I thank the organizations that have helped with research and the necessary publicity. These include over 200 local newspapers, which published my letter appealing for information, and others, from *The Times*, which published my first letter in 1970, to *The Orcadian*, our most northerly newspaper, and almost every other publication in between. Thanks to the Royal Engineers Institute Library, Imperial War Museum, Ministry of Defence Library, Property Services Agency, Royal Armoured Corps Museum and many planning officers of counties and cities who provided information of value. The British Archaeological Trust, who with the British Broadcasting Corporation, recognized the value of the research by awarding the BBC Chronicle Award 1979, which in turn brought more information. Thanks also to Leo Cooper, John Mitchell and Tom Hartman.

Finally in such a project as this, which does 'invade' the home, the help of Celia, my wife, proved the inspiration to complete a task that turned out to be a fifteen-year marathon.

Picture Acknowledgements
Most photos are by author, but thanks are also due to the following individuals: Douglas Baldwin, Mrs Bateman, Peter Connon, John Gamblin, Bill Gent, Olive Hasson, Dennis Hutt, Alfred Pinhorn, Peter Sly, Len Thomas, Viv Trimble, Charles Trollope.

Other illustrations are reproduced by kind permission of Hitchin Museum, the Imperial War Museum, the *Kent Messenger*, *The War*, a publication of the Newnes Group during the war, and *Punch*.

Introduction

PILLBOXES CAME INTO MY LIFE IN 1941 when two were built on the Downton School playing field. They were used as changing rooms by the boys who played their weekly match on that bleak field. The years slipped by and it was not until 1968 that I became aware they were quietly disappearing, the result of roadworks, new building and sinking into the ground. The demolition of one at West Dean, which I had to photograph for the *Salisbury Times*, caused me to inquire why it was sited on the village green and what part it had played in our 1940 defences.

Local inquiries only led to the discovery of more in the locality, but at national level neither the Imperial War Museum, the Royal Engineers Institute nor the Ministry of Defence could supply any details of design or where they were sited. I was referred to the only sketchmap published in *Defence of the UK* by the HMSO, which was not very informative or accurate, the towns of Basingstoke and Aldershot being transposed for a start. It became clear that there was no national record of sites, defence lines or even designs of pillboxes. No doubt the pressure of work in 1940 prevented too much paperwork being filed, and the end of the Defence Regulations and the birth of the Property Services Agency in place of RE Works Services contributed to a clear-out of old documents.

A quick survey of Wiltshire, Dorset and Hampshire showed that enough remained to trace sections of inland defence lines, although not too much was left along the coast. Here much was demolished just after the war and other pillboxes fell over the cliffs. I traced lines through Bournemouth – Salisbury – Warminster and found a good section of the GHQ Line in north Wiltshire. At this point some publicity in the national press and on the radio gave me hope that local archaeological groups would record all Second World War sites and relics in their areas. A few, notably in Kent and Enfield, had already started and have been most helpful.

The very sketchy nature of the information received led me to the conclusion that a nationwide survey, with standard basic information, should be made before any more sites were lost. As no one else appeared on the scene, I decided to undertake this task myself, allowing two years of my spare time. Ten years later the survey reports are still coming in and more than 2000 letters have been written.

The systematic covering of England, Wales and Scotland was begun by dividing it into seven areas and then writing to the local newspapers in each area. Over 200 were written to, with an appeal for information from readers. Around 95% of editors published my letters, sometimes with an article and photo. Readers were offered post-paid survey cards and it is due to some hundreds of them and the interest of editors that the survey ever got started. I eventually recorded the 5,000+ pillboxes and defence sites listed in Appendix B. As the picture of 1940 defences emerged with each completed survey card, other correspondents wrote letters with more details of builders, construction, camouflage and even original blueprints. With so much information to hand, I thought a full account should be published chronicling the efforts of the army and building trade to provide defence against land attack in 1940.

Even now, ten years after my first interest in pillboxes began, I have found few official records remaining; there are gaps, but perhaps someone somewhere may have answers. Until then this is another story from 1940–41, one of the finest periods in our long history.

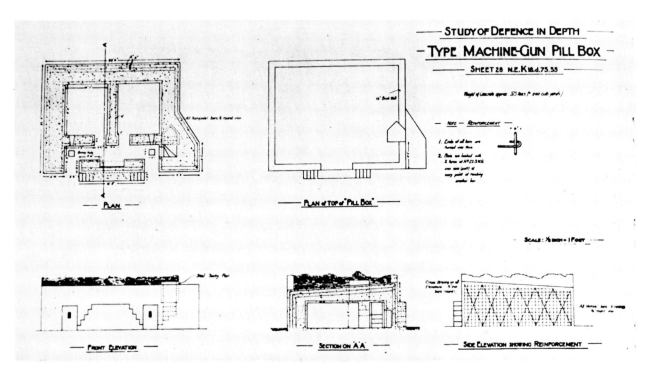

STUDY OF DEFENCE IN DEPTH

TYPE MACHINE-GUN PILL BOX

SHEET 28 N.E. K18.d.75.55

PLAN

PLAN of TOP of "PILL BOX"

FRONT ELEVATION

SECTION ON "A A"

SIDE ELEVATION SHOWING REINFORCEMENT

A German machine gun pillbox of World War I. The rough textured top was to be found on East Anglian pillboxes of 1940.

CHAPTER ONE

Development of the Pillbox until the Second World War

MUCH HAS BEEN WRITTEN about the Battle of Britain as fought in the air between the Royal Air Force and Luftwaffe. The Hurricanes and Spitfires have become symbols of that proud moment in our history. If they had failed, with the Royal Navy unable to intervene, the Battle of Britain would have been continued on land. Then the pillbox would have become another symbol of desperate battles fought along our coasts or, if worse befell, inland.

While the pilots of the opposing forces met in the sky overhead, the British Army and thousands of civilians braced themselves for total war on land. At the threat of German invasion, defence works had first priority, with soldiers and workmen toiling heroically to complete miles of defence line in record time. Pillboxes and 'Dragons' Teeth' had become symbols of impregnable defence, since their virtues had been extolled in magazine and newspaper articles about the Maginot and Siegfried Lines during the 1930s. Coastal defences had been neglected since Queen Victoria's reign, when the last great fortresses were built in Britain. To look at the defence of Britain and development of the pillbox it is necessary to study events since then.

From the Roman forts along the shore to the Tudor coastal forts and, later, Martello Towers, the coast has been the national frontier of the United Kingdom. In later years the Royal Navy was considered the first line of defence. For this reason British forts were built to protect the landward side of naval bases, the key to the fleet's fighting ability. Many remain, in various states of repair, around Portsmouth and Plymouth, which were the nearest points of attack by the French, then the enemy. Specialized emplacements for large guns led to the development of modern fortresses, but the high cost limited the numbers built, only wealthy nations being able to construct the elaborate schemes being designed by the end of the nineteenth century. With the Royal Navy all-powerful, coastal defences stagnated until the First World War.

By now concrete had arrived on the scene as an established building material, a reliable machine-gun had been produced and the Boer War had shown the importance of camouflage. Thus, when war broke out in 1914, new tactics were required by armies trained in mass attacks by cavalry and infantry. The machine-guns inflicted enormous

The circular pattern pillbox of British design, built of individual concrete blocks, located at TG 183405, Norfolk.

The interior of TG 183405, just outside Aylmerton, Norfolk, shows the construction and the sliding steel shutters to the loopholes.

casualties on armies advancing across open country. In the stalemate that developed the artillery bombardment created even more open countryside, but to maintain the effectiveness of the machine-gun it was necessary to have a good field of fire. This meant that some form of protection was needed if the site chosen was in an exposed position. Protection for gun and crew was often a partially demolished house or barn, reinforced with concrete. From this to the purpose-built machine-gun emplacement was a short step. The **Pillbox** had arrived on the battlefield.

When the German Army advanced through Belgium to Ostend in the First World War it was thought possible that an invasion of the United Kingdom could be undertaken by a force of 70,000 men, carried in barges, each holding 500–1200 men. These barges, normally working the Rhine and other inland waterways, would have been escorted by secondary units of the German Navy, while the main units of the British and German navies fought a major battle elsewhere. At the end of 1915 the Royal Navy, weakened by losses and by the Gallipoli operation, could only have intervened in a landing 24–28 hours after the initial attack. It was then thought that up to 135,000 men could have been landed in that period of time. However, by 1917 the number was reduced to the original estimate of 70,000 men made in 1914. With the 24–28 hour delay for naval intervention, the British defence scheme was to prevent the capture of a port in that time. This was as necessary then as now to sustain an invading force. To this end pillboxes were built along the East Coast, some facing inland to defend the ports from an overland attack.

The first British pillboxes were mainly circular in plan and were built of concrete blocks; a number still remain in Norfolk and Suffolk. Pillboxes for the Thames and Medway defences were of the familiar hexagonal type, similar to many built in the Second World War. It was the circular type that gave the emplacement it's name 'pillbox', resembling a box used for pills.

In 1917 the 'Machine-Gun Pillbox' ably demonstrated German skill in the use of reinforced concrete construction and the effectiveness of this 'mini-fort' against infantry attack. The British Army first came up against the pillbox at the Battle of Langemarck on 16 August, 1917, and the official history *War in the Air* records '*Apart from the effectiveness of the new tactical device of the pillbox, for which as yet we have no answer*, the German counterattacks developed without warning.' Larger versions of the pillbox housed artillery, but limited the field of fire and needed plenty of ventilation to get rid of the fumes and smoke. By the end of the First World War concrete had proved itself capable of resisting direct hits by 6-inch and 8-inch shells. Pillboxes could only be overcome by hard fighting, involving the hazardous task of an infantry man throwing a grenade through a loophole. This was a slow process, especially when a number of pillboxes were providing mutual fire support. When the war ended the pillbox had gained a reputation as a good defensive emplacement, especially when concealed and supported by infantry and artillery.

The 1936 Royal Engineers' *Manual of Field Engineering* gives details for the construction of six machine-gun emplacements. The first, built in the shell of a house, incorporates the air space between the walls facing the enemy, in addition to between ceiling and roof. This was designed to absorb the blast of a shell which penetrated the outer wall, while the inner wall gave protection to the occupants. The was a feature of early pillboxes, but was discontinued, as it added complications when construction of large numbers were involved.

The second type (Champagne Type) was a revetted pit, level with the surrounding ground, designed to be used in pairs, connected by an underground passage to a common dugout. As this type required much material and labour it was recommended to be used only for points of special tactical importance. The manual added that they should be used in preference to concrete emplacements wherever possible.

The third, the Reinforced Concrete Machine Emplacement, was of really solid construction, with interior blast wall periscope shaft. It was noted that 3 feet 6 inches of concrete would resist a 6-inch shell.

The fourth, M.G. Emplacement, Breastwork Pattern, was to be part of a trench system. It was to be constructed with concrete in bags, a standard loophole and a corrugated steel ceiling supporting the earth

The 'Moir' Pillbox, one of the inter-war years designs that were pre-fabricated.

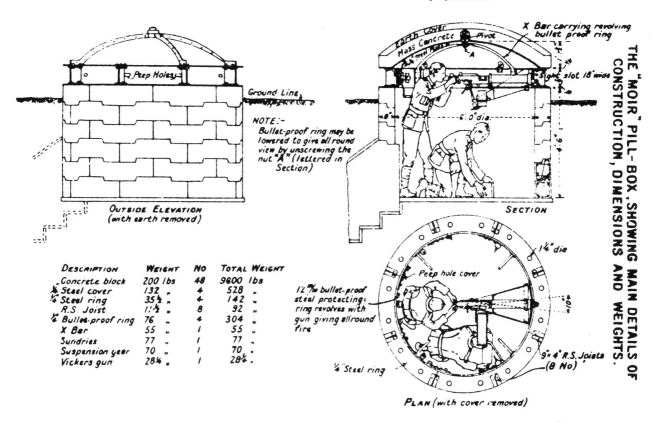

Description	Weight	No	Total Weight
Concrete block	200 lbs	48	9600 lbs
½ Steel cover	132 „	4	528 „
¼ Steel ring	35½ „	4	142 „
R.S. Joist	11½ „	8	92 „
½ Bullet-proof ring	76 „	4	304 „
X Bar	55 „	1	55 „
Sundries	77 „	1	77 „
Suspension gear	70 „	1	70 „
Vickers gun	28¼ „	1	28¼ „

TM 456994 PCNE* — *A World War I pillbox at St Olave's is used as the base of a boatyard office.*

The steel doors still in place on TM 456994.

SU 102314 A/TB — *'Dragons Teeth', the much publicised anti-tank obstacle, built at Wilton to prevent an easy crossing of the River Wylye in 1940. The Official British name, 'Pimple', was a more apt description, although a few vehicles and drivers threatened with a river dip, have appreciated their presence.*

* *The explanation of abbreviations of the shape, construction and type of pillbox is given on p. 73.*

roof. This had a layer of stone-filled sandbags, to burst shells, before they penetrated into the emplacement.

The fifth type was designed to be constructed in four hours, to have the appearance of a traverse and incorporate an air-spaced roof of reinforced concrete. This had the shuttering left in position. A note states that, in the First World War, a direct hit by a 4.2-inch shell smashed the roof, breaking two 3-inch boards, but the crew were uninjured and remained on duty.

The sixth type was designed for a concealed site, where medium protection only was possible. The *Manual* advised reinforcement in which the bars were to be close to the inner and outer surfaces of the wall. This was to prevent penetration by the shell and resist shock, so preventing large pieces of concrete becoming detached inside and injuring the occupants.

The Maginot and Siegfried Lines are outside the scope of this book. However, the 'Dragons' Teeth' of the popular Press and German propaganda ministry were also built in Britain in 1940, under the more prosaic name of 'Pimples'.

Defences between the wars were influenced by armoured warfare, first the ability to stop a tank and secondly to prevent the defence from being overrun by armoured columns exploiting their mobility. For this the anti-tank obstacles, as the first line of defence. These would stop or slow down an armoured thrust, but anti-tank guns were necessary to destroy the tanks. Splinterproof emplacements were considered sufficient by the British. The French housed their artillery in the shellproof works of the Maginot Line. In the facing Siegfried Line (West Wall) the Germans used anti-tank obstacles in depth, with pillboxes in quantity, sited to give mutual fire support. This, then, was the situation at the start of the Second World War.

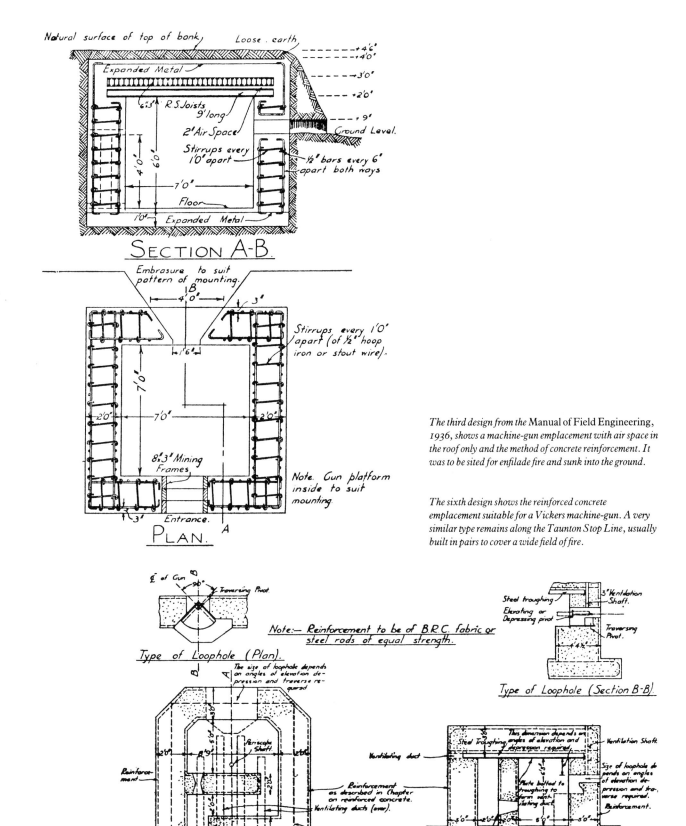

Natural surface of top of bank. Loose earth

- - - - → +4'6"
- - - - → +4'0"
- - - → 3'0"
- - - → +2'0"
- - - → 9"
Ground Level.

Expanded Metal

6'3" R.S.Joists
9' long

2' Air Space

Stirrups every
1'0" apart

½" bars every 6"
apart both ways

4'0" 6'0"

7'0"

Floor

1'0" Expanded Metal.

SECTION A-B.

Embrasure to suit
pattern of mounting.

B
4'0"

3"

Stirrups every 1'0"
apart (of ½" hoop
iron or stout wire).

1'6"

7'0"

2'0" 7'0" 2'0"

8"·3" Mining
Frames

Note. Gun platform
inside to suit
mounting.

3"

Entrance. A

PLAN.

The third design from the Manual of Field Engineering, 1936, shows a machine-gun emplacement with air space in the roof only and the method of concrete reinforcement. It was to be sited for enfilade fire and sunk into the ground.

The sixth design shows the reinforced concrete emplacement suitable for a Vickers machine-gun. A very similar type remains along the Taunton Stop Line, usually built in pairs to cover a wide field of fire.

₵ of Gun 90° Traversing Pivot.

Type of Loophole (Plan).

Note:— Reinforcement to be of B.R.C. fabric or steel rods of equal strength.

Steel troughing 3" Ventilation Shaft.
Elevating or Depressing pivot.
Traversing Pivot.
4'½"

Type of Loophole (Section B-B).

The size of loophole depends
on angles of elevation depression and traverse re-
quired

Periscope Shaft.

2'0" 2'0"

Reinforcement

Reinforcement
as described in Chapter
on reinforced concrete.

Ventilating ducts (over).

Edge of troughing

Plan.

This dimension depends on
angles of elevation and
depression required

Steel Troughing

Ventilation Shaft.

Ventilating duct

Plate bolted to
troughing to
form venti-
lating duct.

Size of loophole de-
pends on angles
of elevation de-
pression and tra-
verse required.

Reinforcement.

5'0" 5'0"

Loophole height as required

Section A-A.

CHAPTER TWO

The Pillbox in Flanders 1939–40

In September, 1939, the British Expeditionary Force arrived in France without a defined operational role. When disembarked, it was decided that the force should defend the Valenciennes – Armentières sector along the Belgian frontier. This was, in fact, the French *Secteur Defensive de Lille*, a sector where the defence works were minimal. At intervals of 800–1000 yds a single pillbox enfiladed the straight stretches of partially finished anti-tank ditch with fire from two-anti-tank guns and one machine-gun. These pillboxes provided protection for weapons and crews from field artillery shellfire. Although designed for use with French weapons, with which the BEF were first equipped, they were successfully modified for use with the British 2pdr anti-tank gun and the Vickers .303 machine-gun.

Having no depth to defences, a scheme based on the French work was produced. This had to be constructed to the rear, as the original works ran too close to the Belgian frontier. It was considered that smaller pillboxes, for one or two anti-tank guns or machine-guns, should be built at the density of six for each kilometre. This target, set by General Gamelin, was reached by 1 and 2 Corps, but 3 Corps on the left, arriving later, did not complete as many.

Fortifications are always a compromise, the balance between wide field of fire and minimum size of loophole for sighting and weapon muzzle being the conflicting requirements. Construction of pillboxes

A pillbox in the British sector, heavily camouflaged, but the elaborate barbed wire perimeter, complete with steel entrance gate negates this concealment. [Imperial War Museum]

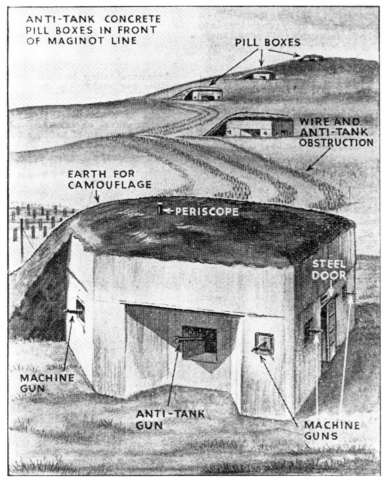

ANTI-TANK CONCRETE PILL BOXES IN FRONT OF MAGINOT LINE

PILL BOXES

WIRE AND ANTI-TANK OBSTRUCTION

EARTH FOR CAMOUFLAGE

PERISCOPE

STEEL DOOR

MACHINE GUN

ANTI-TANK GUN

MACHINE GUNS

Pillboxes in the Maginot Line as depicted by an artist for The War, *a weekly magazine published by Newnes. They were sited for enfillading fire, using an earth bank for protection from direct fire.*

were simplified by using five basic designs for various weapons and sites. They were produced by the Engineer-in-Chief, BEF, and were approved by the Commander-in-Chief, but modifications were allowed by units for special conditions. The designs that were issued for anti-tank weapons incorporated a 30° traverse and similar elevation. This decided the size of the loophole, being based on the French Army's extensive trials during the planning of the Maginot Line. The use of a muzzle pivot-mounting for machine-guns could reduce the loophole needed, thus reducing their vulnerability to enemy fire.

Armour-plate closures were ordered from the UK, but deliveries were late and they had to be grouted in later. While successful experiments were carried out with muzzle pivot-mounting for machine-guns, only a few were incorporated in BEF pillboxes. Again, decisions on loophole design were made difficult as the mountings could not be made compatible with French weapons. At this stage approaches were made to the French for a similar dual capacity in the pillboxes they were constructing, as there was a possibility of unit interchange at that time.

7

Realistic camouflage on an extension to a barn at Mouchin, hides one of the BEF pillboxes. [Imperial War Museum]

SU 309385 PM36 — The Turnbull muzzle pivot mountings for Vickers .303 machine-guns remain in this pillbox at Middle Wallop airfield, the site having been listed by the Department of the Environment.

SU 309385 PM36 — An interior view of a Turnbull mounting, which featured a traverse lock and screw elevation.

With the design settled, construction by Force 'X', commanded by Brigadier A. Minnis, began. This force was the 'brainchild' of the Secretary of State for War, Leslie Hore Belisha, and consisted of five Field Companies and one Field Park Company of the Royal Engineers with the task of constructing defences comparable to the Maginot Line in the BEF sector. This was an impossibility in the time available and not militarily desirable. Arrival of the force did, however, permit the mass-production of pillboxes to begin and re-usuable steel shuttering based on a standard design was ordered from the UK. This was used together with the wooden shuttering made by the Field Park Company, whose workshops also produced steel reinforcing bars of the correct shape and size. With this organization, pillbox erection speeded up, material being supplied by RE Works and Services. Some delays were caused by the limited rail transport available for aggregate for concrete, which slowed the programme by not delivering enough stone to keep pace with construction needs. Despite the difficulties, and despite political interference when the BEF was criticized for slow construction in a political storm which the Press nicknamed the 'Pillbox Row', the overall production was many times greater than that of the French forces. On one French Army front a pillbox was completed every two days.

In the seven months before the German *Blitzkrieg* over 400 pillboxes had been completed in the BEF sector. Rivers and canals were used to supplement the forty miles of anti-tank ditch which had been excavated. Weapon pits for two or three infantrymen were dug wherever possible, but in Flanders' low-lying countryside they could not always be dug to the full depth. Breastworks were then constructed above ground level.

All this effort was in vain, as the German Army by-passed the Maginot Line and little use was made of the pillboxes by the BEF in the Battle of France. Little information, if any, about the importance of the pillbox on the modern battlefield seems to have reached the War Office or GHQ Home Forces. After the Dunkirk evacuation the scene was set for the Battle of Britain.

Plans for the Defence of Britain 1940

IN MAY, 1940, THE Chiefs of Staff decided that, should France fall, air attack would be Britain's first threat. Would the UK be able to hold out against Germany if such an attack was successful? With the population prepared to fight a total war, it was thought Britain would survive.

Enemy activity in France precluded an invasion for some weeks, as time was essential to assemble forces, supplies and ships. This could, of course, be done while the initial air attacks prepared the way for invasion. The Air Staff thought that 5,000 paratroops could put seven key airfields out of action during the vital early stages of a seaborne landing, while 20,000 men with armoured fighting vehicles could land over beaches and deploy inland. Similar thoughts in 1914 had estimated that 70,000 men could be expected and, again in 1940, there were doubts about small naval craft and coastal defences being able to prevent a landing.

On 10 May the Home Defence Executive was set up under General Sir Edmund Ironside, Commander-in-Chief Home Forces, to deal with all matters of home defence. Militarily the threat still had to be defined, but it was considered that serious landings, as opposed to diversionary raids, would only be made on the 500 miles of coastline within range of dive bombers. The evacuation of the BEF from Dunkirk between 27 May and 4 June and the subsequent fall of France brought the situation sharply into focus.

By 7 June Ironside was writing in his diary that all his previous diaries should be sent to Canada, as 'There is no use their remaining in Higham to be overrun'. It would seem that confidence at the top was certainly lacking about the outcome of an invasion. The next day he noted that the Luftwaffe, *after* winning air superiority, could airlift 9,750 lightly armed men on one flight, with the possibility of one and a half flights per day to East Anglia or three flights per day to Kent. At this time, having to rely on ill-equipped troops who lacked mobility, he and his staff completed a defence plan by which London and the Midlands were protected with the GHQ Line and a series of command, corps and divisional stop-lines were sited between it and the coast. By 12 June the country was divided into lines of defence, with defended village and river lines in all directions.

During an inspection at Northolt airfield, Ironside noted good

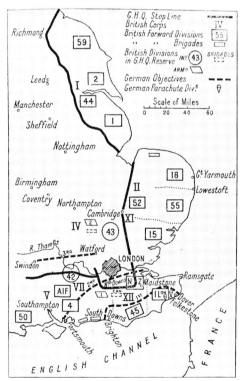

General Ironside's dispositions to meet the promised German invasion of Britain.

*The map shows planned GHQ line (solid)
and other stop lines.*

defences, but was sad to see 2,000 unarmed airmen who should have
been able to take an active part in their own defence. He noted in his
diary that town and borough councils should start defence works,
remarking that it was 'stupid to repair roads, trim hedges and grass,
when pillboxes are needed'. Visiting King's Lynn and Cromer, where
wire was being erected, he commented that the work would never
end: 'It ought to have begun months ago'. He remarked upon the
great failure to realize that all nodal points inland should be fitted with
blockhouses to cover large blocks and so prevent enemy columns
rushing about the country, should a defence line be penetrated. He

10

advocated de-centralization to lesser commanders and involving *all* civilian contractors in work without 'frills'. One bottleneck was the allotment of work by the military, who were liable to make a fuss about intricate reconnaisance and never get the work done.

Ironside's plans were put to the Chief's of Staff on 25 June and Winston Churchill stated that 'on the whole they stood approved'. It was these plans which led to the construction of the thousands of pillboxes and anti-tank blocks, many of which remain to remind us of one of the greatest years in our history. Churchill was shocked to learn that only 57,000 civilians were working on defences and said that the large numbers of troops employed on these tasks should be training eight hours a day.

The first line of Ironside's plan was the 'extended crust' along probable invasion beaches, to beat off minor attacks or delay and canalize penetrations. These troops were to fight where they stood, to gain time for mobile troops to arrive and counterattack immediately.

The second line of road blocks, manned by the Home Guard, were sited at all defiles and nodal points, where they would stop or delay German armoured columns. The Home Guard were to harry any penetration by the enemy and obstacles of every type were devised; flame fougasses and 'Molotov Cocktails' for use at road blocks were favourites. It was in this zone between coasts and GHQ Line that the stop-lines created smaller zones to contain any enemy penetrations inland.

Finally there was the GHQ Line to cover London and the Midlands, this being the last line of defence protecting the Capital and the industrial areas. At this time there were three infantry and one armoured divisions placed to deal with a major breakthrough. Small mobile reserves were in existence for paratroop and minor break-through counterattacks.

The GHQ Line followed natural and artificial waterways, using topographical features where possible, to create a continuous anti-tank obstacle. It contained a heavy concentration of defence works with pillboxes for rifle, machine-gun and anti-tank fire.

Three sections of the GHQ Line for which details are known are as follows: GHQ stop-line Red; Great Somerford to Tilehurst – sixty-eight miles, with 186 shell-proof pillboxes, eleven anti-tank emplacements and seventeen miles of anti-tank ditches. GHQ stop-line Blue; Bradford-on-Avon to Burghfield Mill (Tilehurst) – fifty-eight miles, with 170 shell-proof pillboxes, fifteen anti-tank emplacements and five miles of anti-tank ditches.

GHQ stop-line Green; Highbridge to Freshford then to Stroud to a point six miles SW of Gloucester – ninety-one miles, with 319 pillboxes (forty-eight to be bullet-proof only) and twenty miles of anti-tank ditches. This was also known as the Bristol Outer Defence Line.

These sections were all in Southern Command and this is the only detailed list of GHQ Line defences that exists, as only that Command's papers survive in the Public Record Office. In addition to the

The 'coastal crust' comprised pillboxes such as this Type 22 Milford on Sea, Hampshire, together with mined beaches and obstructed exits. SZ 288914 PCS.

Inland pillboxes were sited to cover railway bridges and embankments, which were used at anti-tank barriers. SZ 194946 DMSW, Hinton Admiral, Hampshire.

Pillboxes situated under a road bridge, cover a railway line at Redbridge, Southampton. SU 370137 RMN and RMS.

main GHQ Line there were command and corps stop-lines. Southern Command's stop-lines are listed as follows: Taunton Stop-line, Bridgwater to Seaton; Salisbury Stop-line, Frome to Salisbury and then to Odiham; Ringwood Stop-line, Christchurch to Salisbury; Oxford Stop-line, Abingdon to Banbury. Within Southern Command the corps stop-lines were as follows; Stalbridge–Blandford–Wimborne to Christchurch; Totton–Romsey–Michelmersh–Chichester–Midhurst to Petersfield and, finally, Wadebridge–Bodmin to Fowey. In addition the beach defences included 247 shellproof and 805 bullet-proof pillboxes, together with forty anti-tank guns and eighty naval guns. This information was recorded in a situation report to GHQ Home Forces on 4 November, 1940.

Other command stop-lines were along the rivers Wye, Tyne, Wansbeck and Coquet. The naval bases at Forth, Scapa, Invergordon, Orkney, Shetland and the Thames and Medway all had defence schemes prepared or modified at this time.

On 26 June an event of importance to future defences was the appointment of General Alan Brooke to be the General Officer Commanding-in-Chief of Southern Command. This was the command responsible for the defence of Southern England, which had become a high risk area after the French coast fell into German hands. On taking command, Brooke's main worry was the shortage of equipment, finding on a vulnerable five miles of coast at St Margaret's Bay, near Dover, only three anti-tank guns, each with six rounds of ammunition. During the next week he was most concerned with coastal defences, the channel being considered our best anti-tank ditch!

Ironside wrote in his diary on 29 June that it had been decided to hold the coast as a 'crust'. Work was proceeding fast on anti-tank obstacles on the beaches. Wire and pillboxes were being erected. Local static defence by armed riflemen, using roadblocks and

12

A small airfield pillbox which had an anti-aircraft gun mounting on top was one of the many varieties used by the Air Ministry in defence of these strategic targets.
SP *298057 Brize Norton, Oxfordshire.*

pillboxes, was being set up all over the country. The GHQ Line was to be manned chiefly by the Home Guard. On 14 July he remarked that at Coventry much had been done to protect the city and make it into a tank-proof island. On the 16th he visited Corsham where much defence work had been done, then lunched at Wilton with Brooke. Writing on 19 July, he said, 'We must get the Home Army organized at once into: 1: Coast Defence and reserves. 2: Striking Columns. 3: Anti-parachute Columns.' On that same day, at 2.45pm, he was told he would be replaced by General Alan Brooke. Anthony Eden told Brooke that he was to take over command of Home Forces at once. Ironside was retired, made a Field-Marshal and given a peerage.

This change was immediately reflected in the defence plans. Brooke moved to his headquarters at St Paul's School, Hammersmith on 20 July, organizing his mobile reserves near the coast to attack enemy landings as soon as they occurred. In this his thinking was along the lines of Winston Churchill, who was advocating the formation of well-armed units of 'Leopards', his name for storm troops later known as Commandos.

A pillbox covering the Royal Military Canal, Appledore, Kent. A water barrier for tanks and transport from a possible beach head. TQ *957292* PCS.

On 30 August Churchill, writing to General Ismay, asked to be informed of the real lines of defence drawn up between Dover, London and Harwich: 'Now that the coast there is finished, there is no reason why we should not develop these lines, which in no way detract from the principle of vehement counter-attack.' At this time consideration was given to a moderate scale of defence for principal harbours against attack from the rear. This explains the siting of pillboxes on the outskirts of such harbour towns facing *inland*. Again this repeats a feature of the anti-invasion defences of the First World War in East Anglia.

Brooke was in total disagreement with concrete road blocks sited at the entrances to towns and villages; he felt they would hinder the

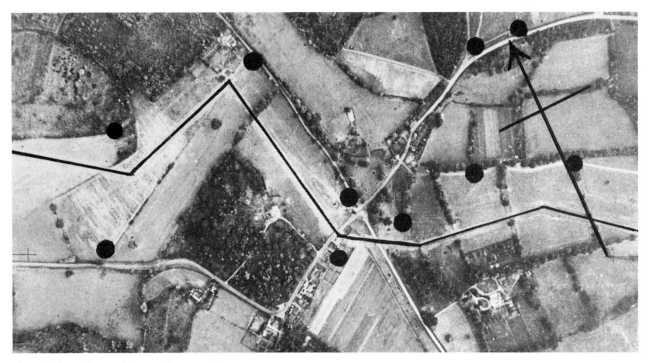

An aerial view of the 1940 defence works at su 796501 Crondall, Hampshire, showing the relationship between pillboxes and the anti-tank ditch.

One of the pillboxes that received the extra reinforcement below loophole level, to bring the total thickness to 3 ft 6 in. TL 660658 PMS, at Newmarket, Cambridgeshire.

mobility of the defenders, so new construction was stopped and many were moved, where possible.

September 7 was the day the 'Cromwell' state-of-readiness order was sent to Eastern and Southern Commands. It was Alert No. 1: invasion imminent and probable within twelve hours. The order caused much confusion, with church bells being run to signify the landing of German paratroops, while in East Anglia several bridges were blown in accordance with the demolition programme. Although a false alarm, it brought a sense of urgency to training and completed pillboxes and emplacements were manned in earnest for the first and last time!

'Sea Lion', the code name given to the German invasion of Britain, was postponed on 12 October, 1940, until the summer of 1941, by which time events in Russia made invasion very unlikely. In May, 1941, GHQ Home Forces asked for a review of pillbox numbers from Eastern and Southern Commands. In June it was thought that the risk of invasion remained and some pillboxes were strengthened, with walls extended to 3 feet 6 inches thick. A few additional ones were built with steel turrets for airfield defence. The Chiefs of Staff agreed on 25 June that a high standard of anti-invasion preparation was still needed, although, eight days earlier, on the 17th, they were saying that no additional work on pillboxes was contemplated, but existing defences should be incorporated into 'centres of resistance'.

By September, 1941, pillboxes were only being built for special purposes and by February, 1942, the Commander-in-Chief directed that no more pillboxes be built.

CHAPTER FOUR

The Design of Pillboxes

THE DESIGN OF PILLBOXES was the responsibility of F W 3, a branch of the directorate of Fortifications and Works at the War Office, whose director in 1940 was Major-General G. B. O. Taylor. This branch issued a series of drawings to the army commands, which in turn issued them to the contractors. The Commander Royal Engineers at the various commands modified them to suit local requirements and materials available. Some of the F W 3 designs were based on those used in France in 1939–40, while others appear to be based on First World War types, such as the hexagonal ones built for the Thames and Medway defences. The designs took the weapon to be used and protection from enemy fire as the main considerations, while standardization was introduced as far as possible to assist mass-construction.

The main infantry weapon of the British Army was the Lee-Enfield .303-inch rifle, and many small hexagonal pillboxes, with walls 15 inches thick, were constructed to give good fields of fire and protection against bullets from rifles and machine-guns.

The Bren gun, the standard light machine-gun, was sited in a larger version of the hexagonal pillbox, some being built with a central well using the gun in it's anti-aircraft role. Pillboxes that were provided with the extra protection of walls 3 feet 6 inches thick were considered shell-proof.

In 1940 the .5-inch Boys anti-tank rifle was the infantry's main anti-tank weapon and it's use from pillboxes was provided for in the design stage by some commands.

The largest pillboxes were for the 2-pounder anti-tank gun, in some cases even a 3-pounder or a 6-pounder, both the latter being weapons of the First World War. The 2-pounder was a highly mobile gun which, with wheels removed and trail splayed, made an effective weapon against the lightly armoured tanks of 1939–40.

The guidelines to thickness and composition of walls needed for defences were rather vague and requirements changed rapidly. In 1939 about half a mile of metre-thick concrete wall and a dozen pillboxes were built near Imber, on Salisbury Plain, to represent the Siegfried Line. Major L. Kitching recalls that it was subjected to artillery fire and infantry attack during exercises.

The most numerous pattern of pillbox, based on the drawings for the F W 3/22, is seen at Great Durnford, Wiltshire. SU 138373 PCW.

A view of the type to the F W 3/23 design shows the anti-aircraft mounting enclosed by a crenellated wall, adjoining the pillbox proper. TL 900470 RCW.

The largest pillbox F W 3/28A, to house the 2-pdr anti-tank gun and Bren guns, is seen at Hungerford, where two of them cover the railway, River Kennet and the Kennet and Avon Canal. SU 351682 RMW.

The Army's 1940 2-pdr anti tank gun emplaced in the pillbox designed for this weapon, by the Royal Artillery's School of Artillery, for a BBC Chronicle film in 1979. Hungerford, Berkshire. SU 351682 RMW.

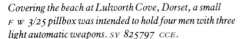

Covering the beach at Lulworth Cove, Dorset, a small F W 3/25 pillbox was intended to hold four men with three light automatic weapons. SY 825797 CCE.

Before this the 1936 *Manual of Field Engineering* gave 3 feet 6 inches as the thickness of reinforced concrete needed to provide protection against a 6-inch shell. To resist a 12-inch shell, 5-feet thickness was thought adequate. This casual approach to research is illustrated in a report by the Ordnance Board in 1940–41 which described the weapon, projectile, range, weather, date, time and target thickness in detail and ended with "Rounds fired – One. Result – Missed". One report issued by Southern Command stated that a 6-pounder emplacement collapsed after the fourth hit during a test firing; no other details were mentioned. Throughout the period of pillbox construction the safety of the occupants was the first concern and increased in the light of new information from home and abroad. At this point it is interesting to note the contents of a captured German report dated December, 1939. This found that, in the campaign against Poland, the standard high explosive shell was useless against reinforced concrete, while 'Anti-concrete' shells from a 150mm gun could penetrate 8 feet of concrete. The great accuracy of the 88mm gun, with it's capability of close grouping, enabled it to penetrate 6 feet 6 inches with eight closely placed armour-piercing shells.

It was not until the Road Research Laboratory, under it's director Dr W. H. (later Sir William) Glanville, started a programme of carefully designed and controlled experiments, from which the formulae for resistance of concrete to projectiles could be calculated, that adequate safety factors could be applied to design. Of course this took time and early pillboxes could not incorporate these factors. By April, 1941, protection demanded included walls to resist an 88mm gun fired from 500 yards, with six rounds in an area 6-feet square, and the roof to be proof from a direct hit by a 250 kilo bomb. This extra protection was to be first applied to anti-tank emplacements. In

September, 1941, the experiments to establish what is an effective pillbox were still in progress, with the testing of reinforced concrete's resistance to 6-pounder anti-tank gunfire.

With the information available to the Directorate of Fortifications in June, 1940, its F W 3 branch issued a series of drawings of pillboxes and reinforcement details to the Army Commands. Copies of some of these original drawings have been found, but reference numbers of others have only survived on official documents, such as accounts and instructions. The numbers and details, where known, are as follows:

F W 3/22   Hexagonal Bren Emplacement; 5 LMGs, 1 Rifle – 6 men.

F W 3/23   Rectangular for land and air defence; 3 LMGs, 1 Rifle – 4 men.

F W 3/24   Hexagonal (one side longer) Bren and Rifle Emplacement; 5 LMGs, 2 Rifles – 8 men.

F W 3/25   Circular concrete Armco Pillbox; 3 light automatics – 4 men.

F W 3/26   Square concrete; 4 LMGs – 5 men.

F W 3/27   Octagon Emplacement. Also F W 3/27A Land and air defence 10 men. A hexagonal pattern of same design was also built.

F W 3/28   Anti-tank 2pdr emplacement. Also F W 3/28A with Bren chamber.

F W 3/29   No details.

F W 3/30   No details.

F W 3/31   Reference to this number for reinforcement details.

F W 3/45   New pillboxes urgently required, to be based on this design.

F W 3/46   New pillboxes by local units to be based on this design.

?????   Sea Wall Pattern pillboxes to be used in Thames and Medway.

All the numbers are referred to as being subject to amendment by the Royal Engineers supervising officers. This was the case in Eastern Command, where, due to the kindness of Hugh Cave, a contractor on the 1940 defences, the complete correspondence on the building of pillboxes in Sectors 8 and 9 of the GHQ Line was made available to me. Here new numbers were used, with F W 3/24 and F W 3/28 being combined to become No350/40, a Bren and Rifle Emplacement. These plans would then be issued to the contractors for the sector, who would then pass them to sub-contractors for individual groups of pillboxes.

In Western Command the CRE issued plans to the Carlisle Garrison Engineer, who in turn passed a copy of F W 3/22 to the Cumberland County Council surveyor, whose department had accepted responsibility for concrete pillboxes at road barrier points, both within highway limits and outside at agreed sites. In the council's archives are retained the county map showing all road barriers erected in Cumberland, together with plans of their own designs for pillboxes. The plans indicate a very individual approach to the problem: all seem to have been circular in plan, built of concrete bags, with loopholes of zinc-coated steel of local design. There are two types of the Cumberland Machine Gun & Anti-Tank Rifle Emplacement, the differences being in the number and type of loophole, but on both plans the provision for a standing or sitting position is portrayed. This

Designed for the Bren light machine-gun, this pillbox to F W 3/24 was built to defend the Royal Navy Depot at West Dean, Wiltshire. SU 283263 PME.

The square pillbox to F W 3/26 is shown with its blast wall to protect the occupants, at South Gare Breakwater, Teeside. NZ 557282 SCE.

The shortage of timber is apparent on this F W 3/26 pillbox; the permanent brick shuttering has remained in good condition since 1940. Happisburgh, Norfolk. TG 368314 SM36.

BROWNING MACHINE GUN EMPLACEMENT.

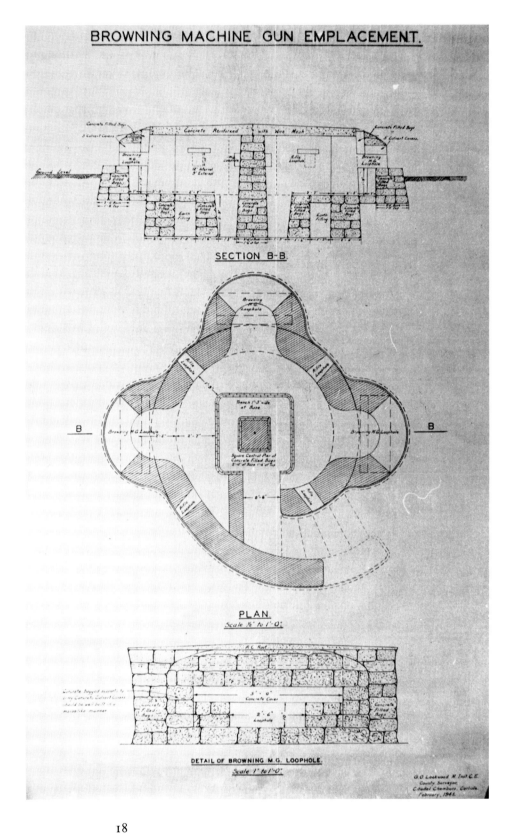

SECTION B-B.

PLAN
Scale ⅛" to 1'-0".

DETAIL OF BROWNING M.G. LOOPHOLE.
Scale 1" to 1'-0".

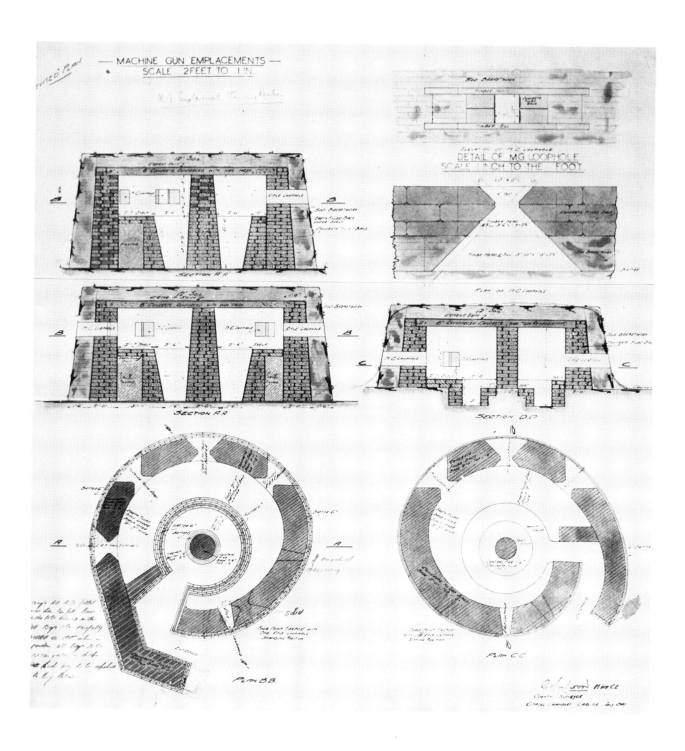

DETAIL OF M.G. LOOPHOLE
SCALE 1 INCH TO THE FOOT

SECTION AA

SECTION BB

SECTION DD

PLAN BB

PLAN CC

Left: In Western Command, Cumberland County Council produced drawings based on official requirements, this one for the Browning machine-gun.

Above: This design for a machine-gun emplacement from Cumberland show two versions; one for standing and the other for sitting firing positions.

19

The Cumberland design near Silloth, Cumbria.
NY 144568 CCNW.

In effect a cast concrete pipe, the Norcon pillbox was basically to the F W 3/25 *design. Weybourne, Norfolk.*
TG 093439 CCN.

The cantilever concrete pillbox, with all-round fire capability, was the product of F.C. Construction Co Ltd who built them at many airfield sites. This one is at Burnaston, Derbyshire. SK 290305.

unique design feature is again repeated in the plans for a couple of machine-gun emplacements, designed by the Cumberland County Council for the Browning Machine Gun in February, 1941. This design, almost clover-leaf in plan, was no doubt due to the issue of the American .300 machine to the Home Guard.

Although the official designs were issued, private companies were quick to offer assistance, especially those with experience of pre-cast concrete. The 'Norcon' pre-cast concrete pipe pillbox was inspected on 18 June, 1940. This was 6 feet in diameter with a 4-inch thick wall of cement fondu, which became bullet-proof in twenty-four hours. It weighed 32 cwt, used no steel and relied on sandbags for internal protection. With a height of 4 feet, it had six loopholes, each 4 × 10 inches, the bottom sill of which was 3 feet above ground. A similar type made by Armco was shown as F W 3/25.

This design was similar, but the walls were 12 inches thick and the roof was 6 inches thick. The cost was £30 each excluding any site work necessary.

Several uses for this type of pillbox were projected, including airfield defence, as extra infantry pillboxes and for Home Guard use on civilian lorries in an *acute emergency!*

The CRE of 18 Division strongly objected to the 'Norcon' type, as it did not provide enough protection. A rectangular type of pillbox was, however, mounted on a lorry chassis and rejoiced in the name of 'Bison' Tank, which, holding ten to twenty men behind 4 inches of reinforced concrete, cost between £150 and £175 to construct.

A more interesting design for a circular pillbox came from F. C. Construction Company Ltd. This featured a concrete cantilevered roof which gave an interrupted 360° field of fire. These were for airfield defence and a few still survive around wartime RAF stations. The company, still in business, was able to supply a copy of the original drawings.

Another circular type, primarily intended for use around or on airfields, was the Pickett-Hamilton Counterbalance Fort, which needed a 'garrison' of five men. One was presumably the commander, as the instructions stated that it took four men about four seconds to raise the 'fort' from it's position flush with the surface of the ground into the exposed position for action. The 'fort' could be lowered in about ten seconds, thereby offering no obstruction to aircraft needing to use the airfield. This type of pillbox required 70 cwt of cement, 6½ yds fine aggregate, 12½ yds coarse aggregate, 10 cwt steel reinforcement and 23 cwt of steel in frames and manholes in it's construction. The cost was estimated at between £230–£250. It was later adapted for hydraulic operation. Sites were chosen at Martlesham (3), Ipswich (3), Wattisham (3), North Weald (3), Hornchurch (3), Stapleford (3), Stradishall (3), Honington (3) and Bury St Edmunds (2).

Others were built at Hawkinge, Silloth and Sunderland, examples still being in existence in 1977. After pumping water out of one at Silloth, Peter Connon, a local military archaeologist, succeeded in operating the raising mechanism.

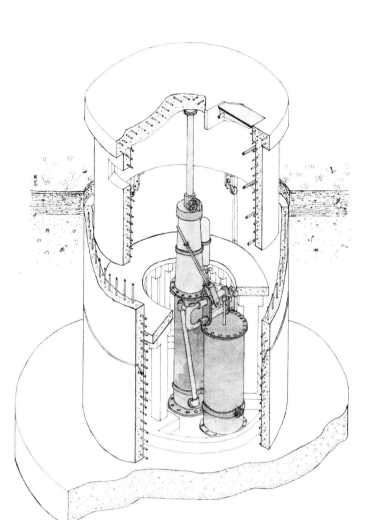

isometric sketch

A drawing to show the mechanism of the Pickett-Hamilton Fort. The raising machinery was based on the standard Sky-Hi garage car lift.

Peter Connon emerges triumphant from the entrance hatch of a Pickett-Hamilton Fort, at the former RAF airfield at Silloth, Cumbria, after finding the raising mechanism in working order after thirty years. NY 112536 P/H.

In fact pre-fabricated pillboxes were being erected as fast as they could be turned out. They were designed to match the potentialities of the materials, rather than follow the official designs. Larger rectangular pillboxes were assembled from concrete slabs bolted together and completed with a roof of the same style. A small circular pillbox was also pre-fabricated in concrete, with a loophole in each section and two concentric rings forming the roof.

Burbidge, builders of East Horsley, Surrey, produced the Tett Turret. This was a small concrete turret on top of a standard 4-foot diameter concrete pipe. It accommodated two riflemen, or a Bren gunner and his No. 2, in rather cramped conditions. The whole was sunk into the ground leaving the revolving top protruding just 13 inches. An enthusiastic brochure from the company suggested that it could be mounted in pillboxes, on the Armadillo or Bison vehicles, but in its designed role, defending road junctions, it would be

21

An example of the rare one-man pillbox, the Tett Turret, at Sudbury, Suffolk. TL 865409 DMS.

The Alan-Williams steel turret was designed for use with most weapons. This one was complete when pictured near Manningtree, Essex.

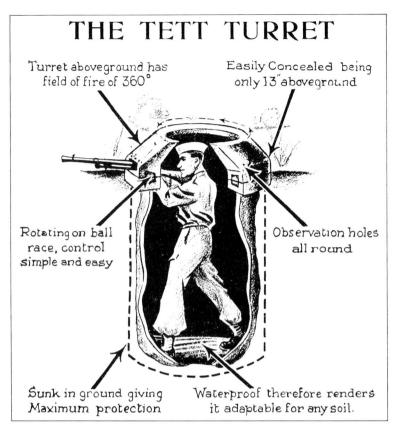

THE TETT TURRET

Turret aboveground has field of fire of 360°

Easily Concealed being only 13″ aboveground

Rotating on ball race, control simple and easy

Observation holes all round

Sunk in ground giving Maximum protection

Waterproof therefore renders it adaptable for any soil.

superior to the normal blockhouse the low profile being its major advantage. However, the Senior Officer RE, Southern Command, found it had a number of serious disadvantages. Entering or leaving through the open top would be a hazardous business with an enemy nearby, and the lack of a cover would mean flooding in any measureable amount of rain. The cramped conditions would mean that it could only be manned for relatively short periods. This, with the problem of entry and exit, would limit its use. Its tactical use would be for airfield defences, road junctions and defence of beach exits. A slit trench was considered to be equally effective in the majority of cases. However, some were built and a few remain in existence.

At the same time the Southern Railway pre-cast concrete works at Ashford produced thousands of loopholes, to be built into pillboxes to speed the work of contractors.

Another type of pre-fabricated defence was the Allan Williams steel turret and, of the 199 ordered, sixty-four were allotted to 2 Corps and 116 to 11 Corps in Eastern Command. Brackets were provided for Bren, Lewis and Lewis anti-aircraft guns and the Boys anti-tank rifle. Similar mountings for the Vickers and the Bren in the anti-aircraft role were promised for October, 1941. Later mountings for the Hotchkiss and Browning machine guns were provided for Home Guard use.

Winston Churchill was asking General Ismay on 12 June, 1940, 'What is being done to reproduce and install small circular pillboxes which can be sunk in the centre of aerodromes, and rise by means of a compressed air bottle to two or three feet elevation, like a small turret commanding the aerodrome?'. He had seen one demonstrated at Langley on a visit during the previous week. Asking for a plan, he thought they appeared to be an admirable means of defence against paratroops.

By far the most widely used design was the hexagonal type, built in two basic sizes, but with many local variations. The F W 3/22, the rifle emplacement, had walls about 8 feet long and 15 inches thick, usually built entirely of reinforced concrete. It had five loopholes and a low entrance often protected by a blast wall. The F W 3/24 version, the Bren or machine-gun emplacement, had walls 10 feet long and up to 3 feet 6 inches thick. This type usually had a 'Y' plan internal wall in addition to the normal exterior blast wall protecting the entrance.

An octagonal type with walls 11 feet 6 inches long was designed with a central well for mounting a Bren or Lewis Gun in the anti-aircraft role. Anti-aircraft weapons were also mounted on the tops of standard pillboxes, where the extra height gave a better field of fire, in particular around airfields and factories.

Square and rectangular types were designed, with the Vickers machine-gun type being the most substantial. These had walls 3 feet 6 inches thick of reinforced concrete and were obviously considered shell-proof. The largest standard pillbox would seem to be the F W 3/28, which housed the 2-pounder anti-tank gun and was built in considerable numbers along the GHQ Line. As these types are still in existence it is possible to make drawings and record details before decay or demolition overtake them. In addition there were many special designs concocted locally for various sites, or indeed various weapons that came to hand. A few naval 3-pounder and 6-pounder guns were used, but whether any anti-tank ammunition was available is another matter. Emplacements for larger weapons are not dealt with, as, being along the shore, they are really coastal artillery and outside the scope of this book.

The protected entrance on a F W 3/24, added in many forms across the country, is shown at Godney, Somerset. ST 486422 PCS.

The Eastern Command design which was based on the F W 3/26, but consisted of a pair of the type joined together to give more space and wider fields of fire. Holkham, Norfolk. TF 891444 SCE.

A gun emplacement for a 6-pdr, designed M A/T 604 on the Taunton Stop Line, near Curry Mallet. ST 317216 RCW. It was the fourth 6-pdr of the Middle Sector.

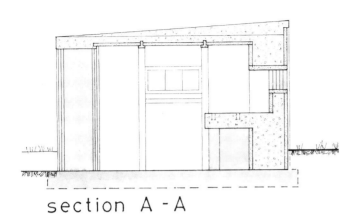

section A - A

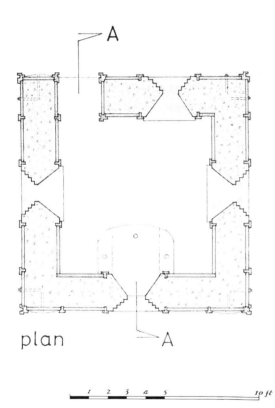

plan

A

A

1 2 3 4 5 10 ft

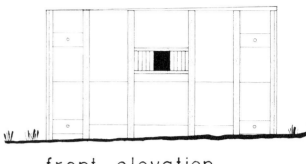

front elevation

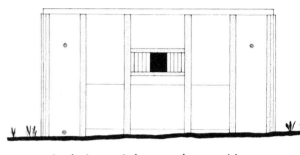

right side elevation

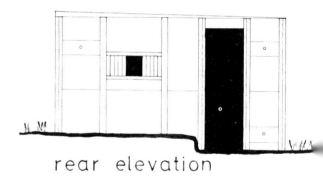

rear elevation

Details of a pre-fabricated pillbox, built from concrete panels bolted together to form shuttering, for the concrete in-fill. Brighstone, Isle of Wight. SZ 412823 RCW.

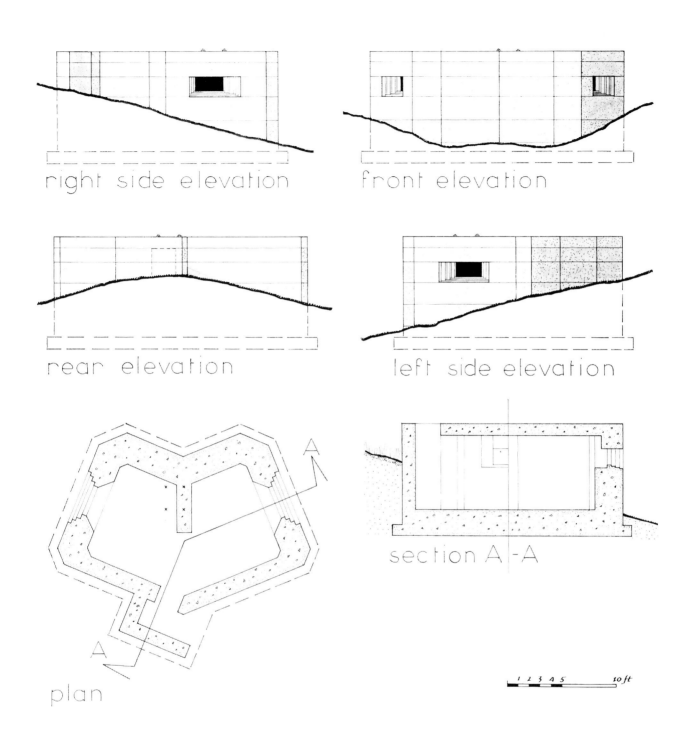

right side elevation

front elevation

rear elevation

left side elevation

plan

section A-A

1 2 3 4 5   10 ft

A twin machine gun post, based on the FW 3/26, for
enfilading fire along the beach at Hemsby, Norfolk.
TG 508174 DCNS.

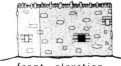
front elevation

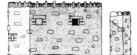

right side elevation

left side elevation

rear elevation

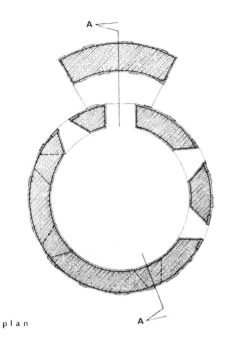
A

plan

A

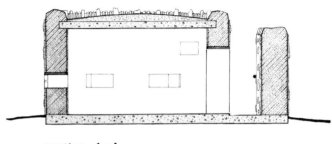
section A-A

scales   plan section   ft
           elevations   ft

The plan of a Welsh 'mini castle'. Holyhead, Anglesey.
SH 261805 CMSE.

26

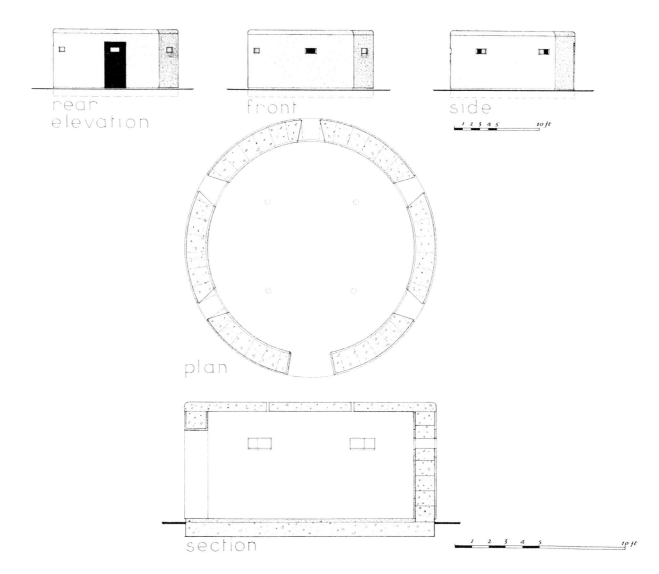

rear
elevation

front

side

1 2 3 4 5   10 ft

plan

section

1 2 3 4 5   10 ft

The circular World War One pattern at Sea Palling,
Norfolk. TG 422269 CCE.

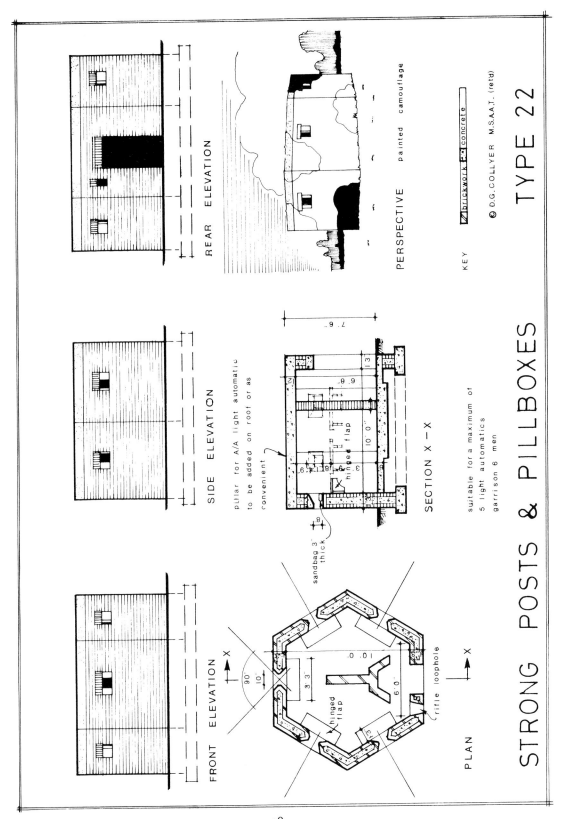

REAR ELEVATION

PERSPECTIVE   painted   camouflage

KEY   ▨brickwork ▨concrete

© D.G.COLLYER M.S.A.A.T. (retd)

TYPE 22

SIDE ELEVATION

pillar for A/A light automatic
to be added on roof or as
convenient

sandbag 3'
thick

hinged flap

SECTION X – X

suitable for a maximum of
5 light automatics
garrison 6 men

FRONT ELEVATION

hinged flap

rifle loophole

PLAN

STRONG POSTS & PILLBOXES

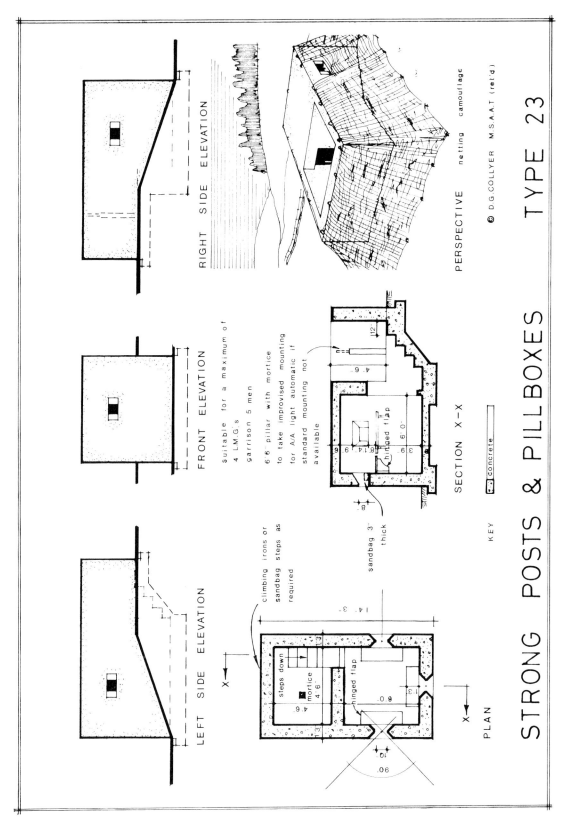

RIGHT SIDE ELEVATION

FRONT ELEVATION

LEFT SIDE ELEVATION

Suitable for a maximum of 4 L.M.G's garrison 5 men

6'6" pillar with mortice to take improvised mounting for A/A light automatic if standard mounting not available

climbing irons or sandbag steps as required

sandbag 3' thick

steps down

mortice

hinged flap

PERSPECTIVE   netting camouflage

© D.G.COLLYER M.S.A.A.T (ret'd)

SECTION X-X

KEY   concrete

PLAN

STRONG POSTS & PILLBOXES

TYPE 23

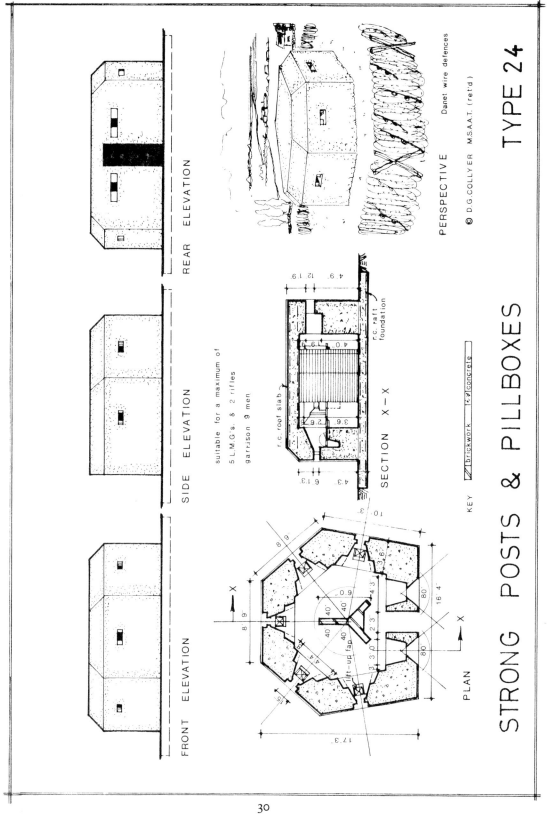

FRONT ELEVATION

SIDE ELEVATION

REAR ELEVATION

suitable for a maximum of

5 L.M.G's. & 2 rifles

garrison 9 men

PERSPECTIVE   Danet wire defences

© D.G.COLLYER M.S.A.A.T. (ret'd)

r.c. roof slab

r.c. raft
foundation

SECTION X — X

12 1 9

4 9

3 6   2 6

4 0   1 9

4 3

6 1 3

PLAN

10 3

8 9

3 6

4 3

0 9

40   40

40

40

2 3

3 0

4 4

8

16 4

80

80

80

17 3

lift-up flap

KEY   brickwork   concrete

STRONG POSTS & PILLBOXES   TYPE 24

30

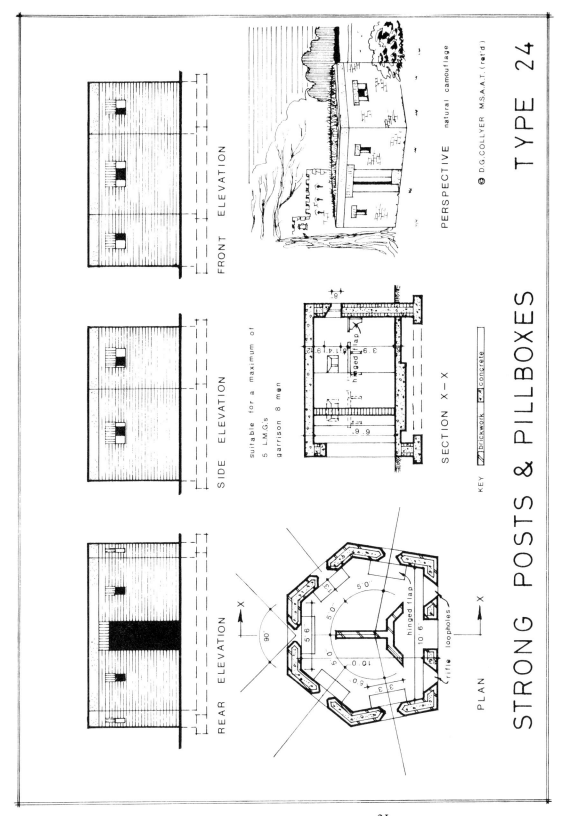

FRONT ELEVATION

SIDE ELEVATION

REAR ELEVATION

PERSPECTIVE   natural camouflage

suitable for a maximum of
5 L.M.G's
garrison 8 men

hinged flap

3' 9"

6' 6"

SECTION X — X

KEY brickwork concrete

90

5' 0"

5' 0"

5' 6"

10' 0"

5' 0"

3' 3"

hinged flap

10' 6"

rifle loopholes

PLAN

© D.G.COLLYER M.S.A.A.T.(ret'd)

TYPE 24

STRONG POSTS & PILLBOXES

31

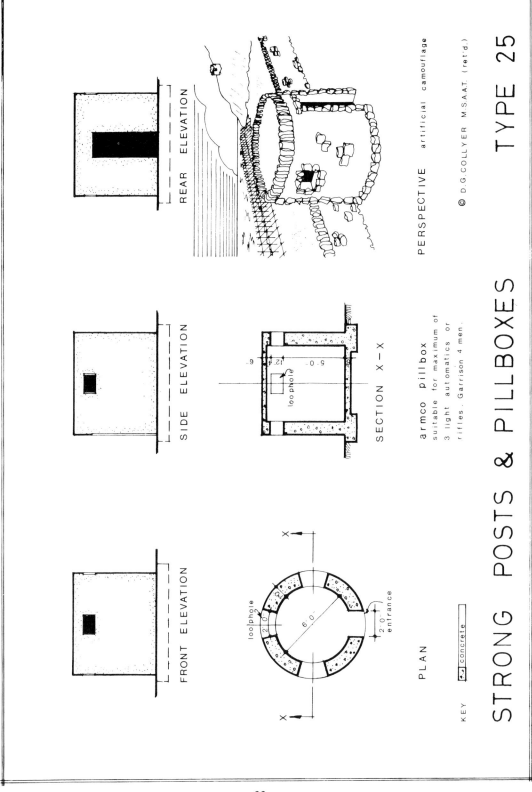

REAR ELEVATION

SIDE ELEVATION

FRONT ELEVATION

SECTION X – X

PLAN

KEY ▪ concrete

loophole

12'4"

5'-0"

6"

loophole

6'-0"

2'-0"

2'-0" entrance

armco pillbox
suitable for maximum of 3 light automatics or rifles. Garrison 4 men.

PERSPECTIVE artificial camouflage

© D.G.COLLYER M.S.A.A.T. (ret'd.)

TYPE 25

STRONG POSTS & PILLBOXES

32

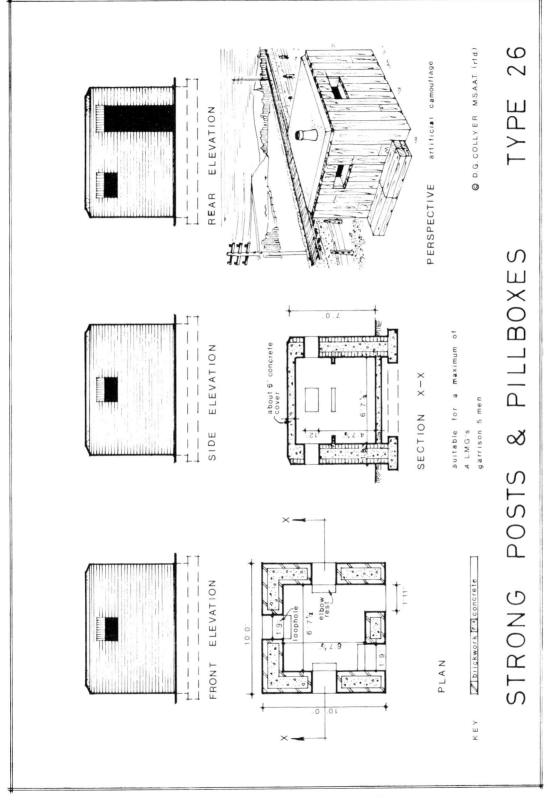

REAR ELEVATION

PERSPECTIVE   artificial camouflage

© D.G.COLLYER M.S.A.A.T. (rtd.)

SIDE ELEVATION

SECTION X-X

suitable for a maximum of
4 L.M.G's
garrison 5 men

about 6" concrete cover

FRONT ELEVATION

PLAN

loophole

elbow rest

KEY   brickwork   concrete

STRONG POSTS & PILLBOXES   TYPE 26

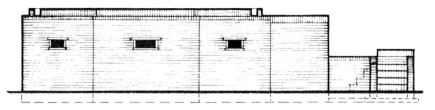

RIGHT SIDE ELEVATION

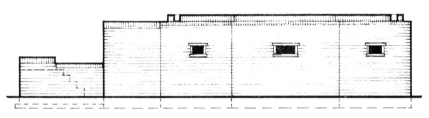

LEFT SIDE ELEVATION

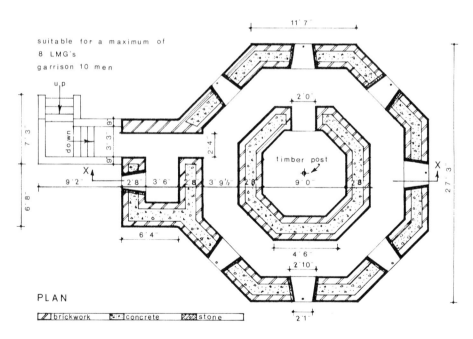

suitable for a maximum of
8 LMG's
garrison 10 men

timber post

PLAN

brickwork   concrete   stone

STRONG POSTS & PILLBOXES   TYPE 27.

© D.G.COLLYER M.S.A.A.T.(ret'd)

SHEET   1.

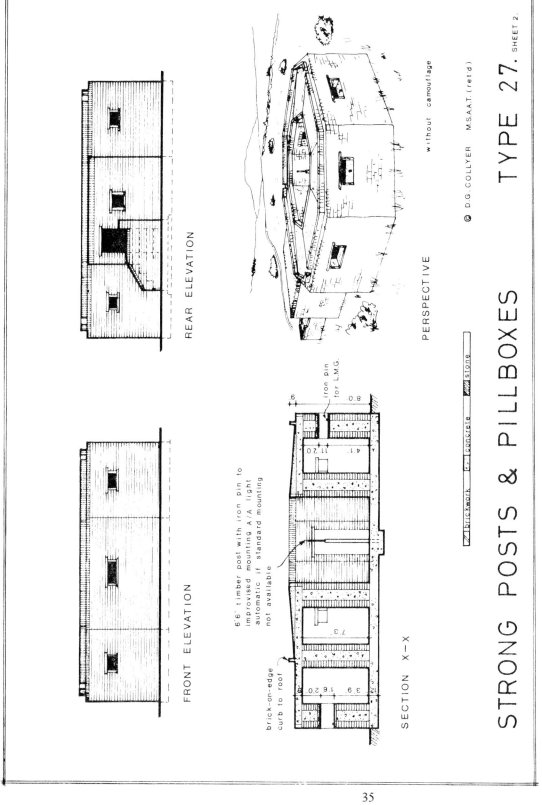

REAR ELEVATION

FRONT ELEVATION

PERSPECTIVE

without camouflage

SECTION X—X

6'6" timber post with iron pin to improvised mounting A/A light automatic if standard mounting not available

iron pin for L.M.G.

brick-on-edge curb to roof

© D.G.COLLYER M.S.A.A.T.(ret'd)

brickwork   concrete   stone

STRONG POSTS & PILLBOXES

TYPE 27. SHEET 2.

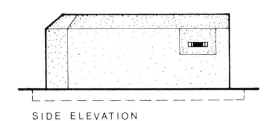

SIDE ELEVATION

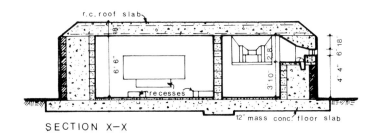

r.c. roof slab

recesses

12" mass conc. floor slab

SECTION X—X

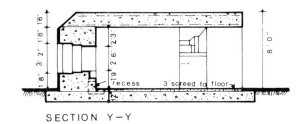

recess   3" screed to floor

SECTION Y—Y

KEY   concrete   conc. blocks   Phorpres blocks

suitable for one 2pdr. A/T

gun and a maximum of 3No.

L.M.G.'s

garrison 10 No. men

STRONG POSTS & PILLBOXES TYPE FW 3/28

SHEET No.1.   © D.G.COLLYER   M.S.A.A.T. (ret'd.)

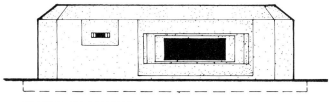

FRONT ELEVATION

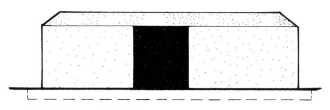

REAR ELEVATION

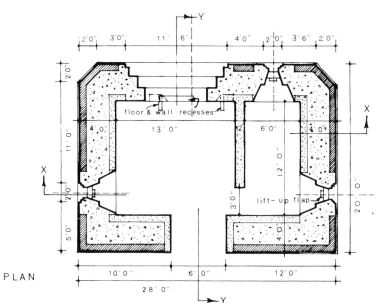

PLAN

STRONG POSTS & PILLBOXES TYPE FW3/28

SHEET No 2   © D.G. COLLYER M.S.A.A.T. (ret'd.)

37

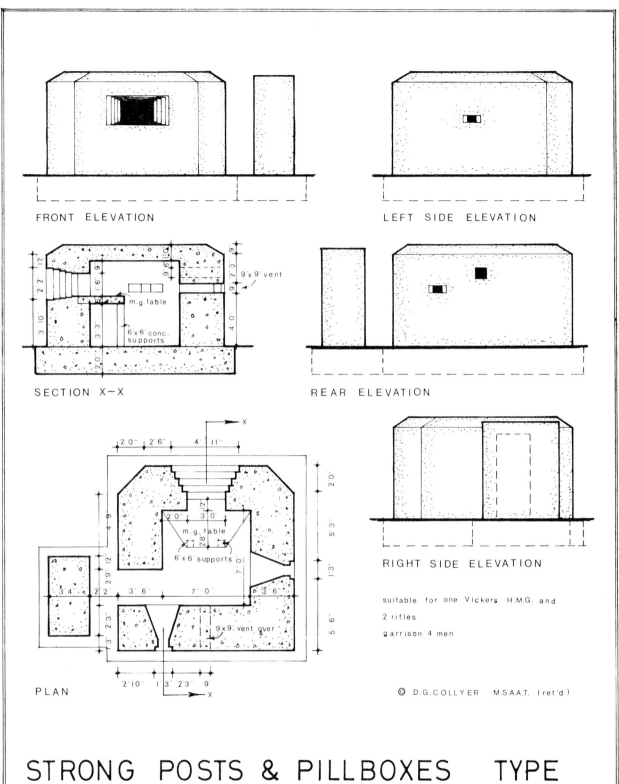

FRONT ELEVATION

LEFT SIDE ELEVATION

SECTION X-X

9"x9" vent

m.g. table

6 x 6 conc.
supports

REAR ELEVATION

PLAN

X

m.g. table

6 x 6 supports

9"x9" vent over

X

RIGHT SIDE ELEVATION

suitable for one Vickers H.M.G. and
2 rifles
garrison 4 men

© D.G.COLLYER   M.S.A.A.T. (ret'd)

STRONG POSTS & PILLBOXES   TYPE

CHAPTER FIVE

The Design of Anti-Tank Obstacles

ALONG WITH PILLBOX DESIGN and construction, anti-tank defences were taking shape. With the desperate shortage of tanks and anti-tank weapons, passive measures were the only ones widely available to prevent mobile German columns running riot over the countryside, after breaking through the coastal "crust".

The first line of defence was, of course, the English Channel, correctly referred to as our most effective "anti-tank ditch". Behind this came the steel scaffolding, mines and concrete blocks of various sizes.

The Manual of Field Engineering (RE) for 1936 did not have any design information on permanent artificial obstacles for tanks. It did, however, lay down guidelines for the construction of "tankproof localities", involving the use of a combination of natural and artificial obstacles, the latter to cover the gaps between the natural tank barriers.

Figures given for use in designing tank obstacles were as follows:

A sketch of the scaffold barrier and concrete blocks on the outskirts of Oulton Broad dated 1st July 1943. It is part of a series by the mother of Miss P. R. Miller, who has recorded sites in Norfolk.

Vertical height of obstacles	3 feet
A slope greater than	45 degrees
A trench wider than	8 feet
Water exceeding in depth	3 feet 6 inches

The manual also added that the figures were liable to modification with the expected improvement in tank performance and must be adapted to the actual performance of enemy tanks. Recommendations given included trees of not less than 9 inches in diameter and not more than 8 feet apart, with stumps cut to 2 feet 3 inches high; 80lb steel rails, 5 feet long, driven into the ground leaving 2 feet 3 inches exposed; rails and sleepers or timber poles, stacked 3 feet wide and high, securely fixed to stakes 4 feet in the ground. The use of ditches, slope and rails, and the bank and pole, were also featured in the drawings. Except in the matter of dimensions, these obstacles still appeared in the 1951 edition of the manual!

By 1940 the press was full of helpful hints on stopping tanks and the construction of road blocks. This was reflected in the early versions,

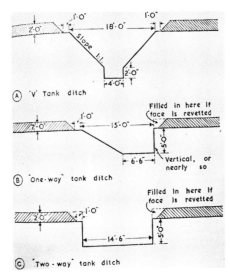

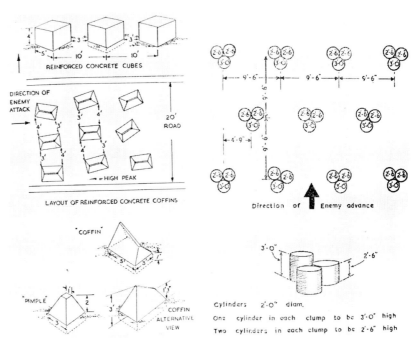

Above: The dimensions and sections of the recommended anti-tank ditches. [Military Manual, 1950]

Centre: Designs of the standard anti-tank obstacles of reinforced concrete. [Military Manual, 1950]

Right: The disposition of concrete cylinders as a road block. [Military Manual, 1950]

where everything, including the kitchen sink, was incorporated in a multitude of local barriers across roads. Other ideas came from the Maginot and Siegfried Lines, the so-called 'dragons' teeth' being shown as impregnable.

In June, 1940, obstacles were considered *the* method of forcing the enemy to stop, thus enabling an aggressive defence to be conducted by local forces as a delaying tactic. A series of such defences would allow the mobile reserves to intercept the thrust and stage a full-scale counter-attack. During their construction, full use was to be made of natural obstacles, such as rivers, marshes and high ground. Where the situation allowed, anti-tank ditches were to be dug. The 'V' type of ditch, thought to be proof against 25-ton tanks, was 12 feet wide at ground level, 5 feet 6 inches deep and used the spoil to make a bank 5 feet 6 inches high on the attackers' side. This gave the enemy an 11 feet drop into the ditch.

Wherever a ditch was impractical, concrete obstacles were to be used, especially along the coast and at road blocks inland. These permanent artificial obstacles followed five basic designs; cubes, blocks (coffins), pyramids (pimples), cylinders and 'buoys'.

The concrete cubes were produced in two sizes, 3 feet 6 inches and 5 feet. Blocks or 'coffins', with a base 5 feet × 3 feet, tapering to a ridge starting 1 foot 3 inches, rising to 3 feet, were more difficult and therefore slower to construct. Few seem to have been built and by 1941, were considered a poor defence against tanks. Two sizes of the pyramids or 'pimples', the British version of 'dragons' teeth', were made, one with a 4-foot square base and the other 3-foot square, while both were 2 feet high. Cylinders also came in two sizes, with those 1

40

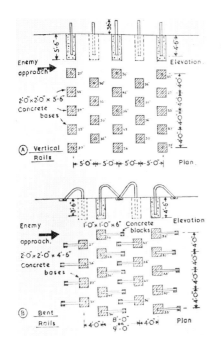

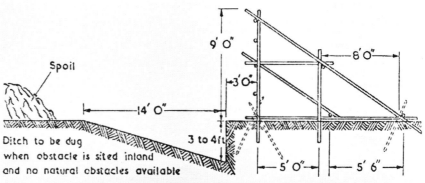

foot 9 inches in diameter being 2 feet high and the others 2 feet in both diameter and height. The final type was the 'buoy', a kind of concrete dumbbell consisting of two concrete cones, with rounded bases, mounted on a steel bar about 6 feet apart. These were not recommended as an obstacle by 1941. Their designed use was to be strewn around in front of steel-rail road blocks. Also by 1941 the 5-feet cubes were discontinued and, from a study of the amounts of material in cubic feet per mile of single obstacles, the reason becomes obvious. Cubes were to be built in double rows, while other obstacles were to be arranged in five rows. The cylinders were usually placed in front of the removable steel rails or RSJs that formed barriers used across roads that had to be kept open for normal users. For this reason they had a steel bar cast in the top, from which a steel wire could join a number together in a road block, thus preventing a tank from moving them one at a time. They were disposed in five rows on the hard road surface and a number of broken bricks were scattered to prevent them being rolled clear easily.

Design	Spaced at centres	Depth in ground	Volume cu.ft Single per mile
3ft 6ins Cube	8ft 6ins	1ft 6ins	38,000
5ft Cube	11ft	1ft 6ins	78,000
4ft 'Pimples'	7ft 6ins	1ft	22,000
3ft 'Pimples'	7ft 6ins	1ft	13,200
2ft Cylinder	6ft	–	5,500
1ft 9ins Cylinder	6ft	–	5,300
'Buoy'	6ft	–	4,400

All that remains of the anti-tank ditches around Salisbury, Wiltshire, are the bridges built for traffic to cross the barriers. This one is at Laverstock. SU 158297 A/TD.

The sea removing sand on the Isle of Grain, Kent reveals the concrete foundations used to keep the Pimples effective against vehicles on soft ground. TQ 887772.

The steel scaffold barrier was erected along the coast by the Royal Engineers, assisted by other arms, towards the end of 1940. This tubular steel scaffold fence was about 9 feet high and as late as 1951 was considered able to stop 35-ton tanks, unless they were able to charge. This would not have been possible on the beach as the barrier was erected near the low-water line, leaving no run-up. There were difficulties in securing the barrier on sand, but these were overcome by the development by Stewart & Lloyd of the sword picket, later known as the 'Wallace Sword', a name adopted officially by the Admiralty. The 'Z1' type of scaffold barrier could be erected quickly, but it used large quantities of steel urgently needed for other purposes. Despite this, many miles of barrier stretched along the coastline of south and east England, using more than 15,000 miles of tube in the process.

In June, 1941, defences were reviewed and revisions made. The 'coffins' were considered a poor anti-tank obstacle. The cubes were to be built edge-on, instead of being square to each other. Cylinders were to be used in threes, with one large and two small, in clusters spaced on 9 feet 6 inch centres. Three or four lines, with the clusters staggered, were recommended for use as a road block, again being repeated in the *1951 Pamphlet No. 2* on *Field Defences and Obstacles*. As mentioned the 'buoys' were out and, surprisingly at this stage of the war, railway wheels were listed as effective material for a block. By now the 'V' type anti-tank ditch was modified to become a 'two-way ditch', with a width of 18 feet at ground level and a depth of 9 feet. Spoil was divided equally between both sides to add an extra 3 feet in height to each bank.

Extensive anti-tank obstacle trials were held at Westbury, near Imber, on 13/14 August, 1941, when a tank equipped with a

A Matilda tank demonstrates the way the rail barriers were supposed to work.

Steel rails still in place in 1983 at Narborough, Norfolk. TF 764144 A/TR×36.

42

WE SHALL DEFEND EVERY TOWN, EVERY VILLAGE, EVERY STREET

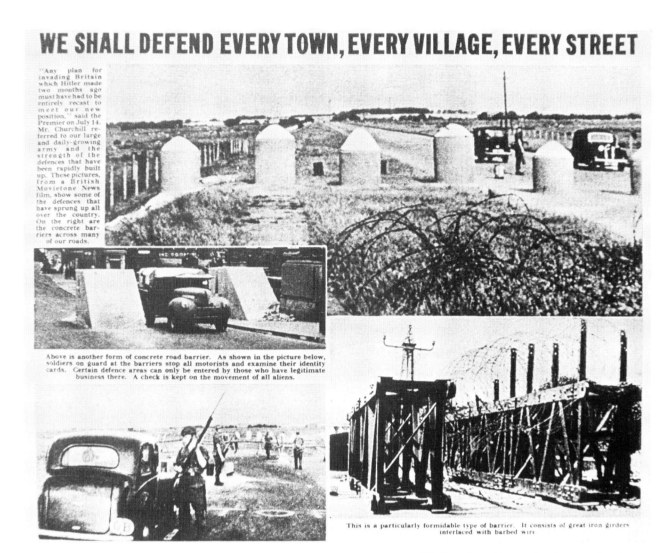

"Any plan for invading Britain which Hitler made two months ago must have had to be entirely recast to meet our new position," said the Premier on July 14. Mr. Churchill referred to our large and daily-growing army and the strength of the defences that have been rapidly built up. These pictures, from a British Movietone News film, show some of the defences that have sprung up all over the country. On the right are the concrete barriers across many of our roads.

Above is another form of concrete road barrier. As shown in the picture below, soldiers on guard at the barriers stop all motorists and examine their identity cards. Certain defence areas can only be entered by those who have legitimate business there. A check is kept on the movement of all aliens.

This is a particularly formidable type of barrier. It consists of great iron girders interlaced with barbed wire.

The War, *the weekly magazine, shows a variety of anti-tank barriers.*

2-pounder gun took part, using live ammunition. The obstacles were: bent rails/RSJs, steel 'hedgehogs', curved steel obstacles, Dannert wire in quantity, cubes, cylinders, 'buoys' and tubular scaffolding. The test was in three phases, with the stationary tank firing at short range, a timed test to demolish the various obstacles and an assault demonstration. The result was that the reinforced concrete cylinders withstood the 2-pounder gunfire best of all, but that anything slowing up the tank helped the defenders. The tank, having to get close to destroy the obstacle, was then within range of the defence's shorter-range weapons. With the invasion of Russia by the German Army in the summer of 1941, the threat of 'Sea Lion' being put into operation became remote, but by then many thousands of concrete blocks dotted the countryside, many remaining forty years later.

As with pillboxes, there were a number of variations from the official pattern, with perhaps the Sussex 'Tombstone' being the most

The timber shortage affected the construction of the anti-tank blocks. These at Dinder, Somerset, show that corrugated iron was used as shuttering material but the removal of shuttering too soon meant a repair job on the right-hand block.

The concrete revetted anti-tank ditch at Pevensey Bay. TQ 641011 A/TD.

unusual. At Taddiford Gap on Hordle Cliff (s z 261923) a double row of cubes and blocks remain (1977). The cubes are 4 feet, plus a pyramid top of 1 foot 3 inches. Some overhang the cliff to show that no foundation was used and that the 6 inches they have sunk into the ground is due to settlement. The few blocks on the site would appear to be double cubes in size. Inscriptions made in the wet concrete are visible on some, with the initials of builders and on one the badge of the Green Howards over the words '6th Batt, Ex B.E.F.'. Another simply states: 'The Last Block, July 31 1940'. At Battle, Sussex, the days' scores by the Royal Air Force in the Battle of Britain were recorded on some obstacles.

At the same time as the anti-tank ditches were being dug, shallow ditches to prevent aircraft and gliders landing were also being incorporated with the other anti-airborne landing devices. Poles were erected over much level open space, including large areas of sand exposed at high tide around the coast. Logs were moored in patterns on the King George V Reservoir at Chingford to prevent seaplane landings. M 10 at the War Office thought tanks could be landed by plane or flying boat!

CHAPTER SIX

Pillbox Construction

TRANSLATING THE FOREGOING DEFENCE plans and pillbox designs into reality was a big task for the military in the first instance and then for the hundreds of British building contractors who joined together in a mammoth undertaking.

Firstly, the Army Commands sent out teams to survey the countryside and recommend suitable defence lines. The Royal Engineers, co-operating with other formations, were responsible for the collection of RE Intelligence, construction of defences and distribution of engineer stores, which included the necessary barbed wire, etc. At this time the Army shared the defence of the airfields with the Royal Air Force, which must have seriously overburdened the Fortification and Works Branch of the Royal Engineers. RE Intelligence included the selection of bridges and other military objectives of use to the enemy for demolition. These were chosen during reconnaissance for the defence lines and the preparations were carried out immediately by RE units, especially where road bridges were concerned.

Authority for entry to private land for the building of pillboxes and other defence works was provided under Regulation 50 of the Defence Regulations, 1939, and the basis for compensation was the annual diminution in the value of the land. For example, a 10-acre field with an annual value of £10 and a pillbox in the corner, may have diminished in value by 5/- per annum. If it was necessary to have a barbed wire protection enclosing 2 acres, the annual payment might be £2 per annum. Compensation was paid quarterly, until such time as the works were no longer required, when notice to terminate the agreement was served. The owner could then claim damages up to the capital value of the site. By 1960 the Defence Regulations were cancelled and any site claims not settled earlier were dealt with and payment made to the current owner under the Compensation (Defence) Act, 1939.

In the construction of pillboxes the local Commander Royal Engineers issued orders to local contractors to provide forthwith '. . . the labour and materials required in the erection and completion of pillboxes according to Drawings 27,28,29 and 30, amendment under the Anti-Tank Defence line R.E. Supervising Officers'. This order

Due to the timber shortage for shuttering during the building of the concrete pillboxes, the War Office approved the use of bricks as a form of permanent shuttering on the exterior. Here, Phorpres hollow bricks have been used at Boyton, Wiltshire. ST 954404 PMS.

Mrs Olive Hasson (right) the photographer, and her niece sit in the 2-pdr anti-tank gun embrasure of the F W 3/28A pillbox under construction in her garden at Theale, Berkshire. SU 647705 RCS.

A view of the F W 3/28A, showing the steel reinforcing rods and the formwork in place to mould the standard Bren loophole. SU 647705 RCS.

A reminder that building in 1940 was not the mechanised operation it is now. The portable concrete mixer was the only help in preparing tons of concrete used in defence work. This is one of a series of pictures taken of a F W 3/28A under construction at Theale, Berkshire. SU 647705 RCS.

was the standard form sent to contractors and informed them that they would be paid according to prices set down in the 'Form of Prime Cost Contract for Emergency Works'. A footnote requested that the contractor should read this form, which could be obtained from His Majesty's Stationery Office, price 5d post free.

It was at this time, in May, 1940, that Major-General A. G. B. Buchanan RE recalled ringing a big building contractor to ask if he could undertake the building of 200 pillboxes along fifty miles of coast in *three* weeks. This was the speed of events. Much of the negotiating with contractors was completed by the time RE Intelligence had provided the information on the siting. In getting this information, the Royal Navy's advice on the suitability of beaches for a military landing was sought, those most likely to be used getting first priority.

One of the original orders for defence works, dated 24 June, 1940, serial W.O.34664, has survived, thanks to Hugh Cave of Thorney, near Peterborough, and gives the full story of construction in two sectors of the GHQ Line. This order from His Majesty's Principal Secretary of State for the War Department required the attachment of a 6d agreement stamp and was to be returned to the CRE East Anglia. Mr Cave also received a list of charges to be made when preparing accounts for the construction of pillboxes in Sectors 8 and 9 of the GHQ Line and at searchlight units in the Areas 216 and 219. These make interesting reading and are reproduced.

By early July the tremendous amount of defence work and other wartime construction had caused such serious inroads to stocks of cement that the Director of Fortifications and Works sent a memorandum, *Economy of Cement in Defence Posts*, to all Chief Engineers of the Home Commands. The measures to be adopted, where practical, were that for floors on a good firm sub-soil the strength of concrete should be reduced to a 1:3½:8 mix (1 part cement: 3½ parts sand: 8 parts aggregate) instead or the normal 1:2:4 mix. The thickness was to be reduced to a minimum, of the floor omitted if possible. Where enemy fire was expected, the walls were to be the 1:2:4 mix, with the full thickness retained. For walls not so exposed, a 1:3:6 mix, or a 9-inch brick wall with earth or rubble backing, was considered sufficient. Defence posts were to be sited with floors below ground level, allowing for field of fire and drainage. Walls below ground level were to be built without reinforcement and with the maximum economy in the use of cement. Bricks, pre-cast concrete units, stone or breeze blocks could be used for walls below ground level, with a lime mortar in place of cement mortar, using a 1:3 mix. This mix was recommended for the brickwork used as shuttering for concrete walls. This accounts for pillboxes now standing with a rough concrete finish, where, with the passage of time, the brickwork has fallen to expose the reinforced concrete.

At Thorney work began on 21 June, 1940, with contractors working a seven-day week for five weeks, averaging a twelve-hour day, and then a further six weeks of normal working. Throughout this period Mr Cave, as the group contractor, was responsible for the work of his sub-contractors in the surrounding area. Together they built seven Type 24, four Type 27A, three Type 28A and eleven Type 340/40 pillboxes, these with their associated road blocks. There were difficulties to be overcome during construction, as the sites were chosen for military use rather than the convenience of contractors.

The Pillbox at Hailley's Farm, North Warnborough, Hampshire is now hidden under the barn, but the complete list of materials used in its construction and that of the adjacent pillbox at Walnut Tree Cottage survives. SU 729511 DCNW.

This pillbox at Pirbright, Hampshire, shows the uneven roof incorporated during construction as part of the camouflage scheme. Sometimes buckets of concrete were turned out by the builders, in the manner of sandcastles. SU 932562 PC36.

47

A partially demolished pillbox at Milford-on-Sea, Hampshire, showing the roof reinforcement for a standard F W 3/24 pillbox. SZ 295912 PCS.

List of charges to be made when preparing accounts for erecting pillboxes in Sectors 8 & 9 GHQ Line and at searchlight units in Areas 216 & 219.

Materials:

Gravel. Sand. Bricks: pressed cants, squints, bats.	(£1/16/0 per 1,000)
Cement. Lime. Water.	According to cost. (2/8/6d. per ton – 5/- refund for paper sacks)
Timber for shuttering.	Invoice price less valuation (4/- per cu. ft.)
Timber for loopholes	Invoice price less firewood price (£1 ton)

Reinforcement: Only chargeable where purchased by builder.
Timber shelves at current price.
Camouflage materials: including paint, corrugated iron, timber for doors and windows, wire netting and straw at invoice price.

Plant & machinery:

Concrete mixer (hours worked)	5/3 1od. per hour.
	7/5 1/3d. per hour.
Rod bender	8/- per week
Rod Cutter	1o/- per week
Woodworking machinery (hours worked)	4/- per hour + machinist's time.

Labour:

Foreman (one only allowed)
Bricklayers, carpenters and painters; chargeable at rate (1/5d. per hour).
Labourers; chargeable at rate (1/2d. per hour).
Apprentices; as paid and full overtime rates.
National Health & Unemployment Insurance.
Workmen's Compensation, rates on total.
Public liability, rates on total.

Haulage:

Materials to site
Lorry taking workmen to site 1/- per mile
Car taking workmen to site   6d. per mile over 4 miles from town.
                              9d. per mile with trailer
Allowance for plant and tackle over 5 miles from town 1/- per mile.
Bus fares.
(petrol 1/9d. per gallon)

Sundries:

Nails, screws, wire, oil & petrol for mixers.
Tarpaulins 5/- per week.
Shed on site 7/6d. per week.
Hand pump 12/6d. per week.
Petrol pump £2/1o/od. per week.
Baulks for temporary roadways 2/- each per week.

After completion of the work a series of letters passed between the contractors and F W 6, the Billing Section of Home Defence Works Services at the War Office, which continued until July, 1941. F W 6, querying Final Bill No. 1573, assumed that the contractors would accept their alterations and reductions: 'In the interests of National economy, it is expected you will agree to the very reasonable amendments required, remembering that this work had necessarily to be carried out in a time of National Emergency in the defence of our Country'. They were alarmed to find the total cost for Mr Cave's work was £2,852 2s 8d; it was decided 'by technical calculation and experience of the department by examination of some 1,000 bills that the cost should be £1,211'.

In reply Mr Cave stated that he did not agree to reductions in his workmen's travelling expenses and pointed out that his agent's travel was reasonable, when considering the amount of time and travel necessary to complete work spread over a large area quickly. He indicated the high cost of one site at Welches Dam, but had been told the site was fixed and must be completed regardless of cost. Requesting that F W 6 refer to details of work done, he thought they would not find the cost so alarming. He ended, 'We are fully aware of the necessity of National Economy and certainly do all we can to help this on. We did not hesitate when called upon to carry out this Emergency Work and certainly did not wait to see if we were going to be paid for what we did, but put all our resources at the disposal of the War Department.'

All was eventually settled, but the difficulties at Welches Dam illustrate what must have faced contractors up and down the country when they tried to meet the military requirements.

The Welches Dam site was twenty-five miles from the Thorney depot of H. & L. Cave, which obviously added to the cost. It was situated 400 yards along a narrow river bank between two rivers, requiring the laying of a light railway on top of the bank. This was removed from a distant site and conveyed to Welches Dam by barge. All materials for construction were off-loaded at the railhead and carried to the site on trucks. A Type 28 anti-tank emplacement and Bren chamber was to be sited on top of the bank, with work beginning on the 11-foot deep foundations. But alterations were made by the RE Officer on the site. He designed a reinforced saddle foundation and did not include a Bren chamber in the finished emplacement. In addition, two other pillboxes were built on the site to give supporting fire, one for Bren guns and the other for rifles. Owing to the danger of flooding, the Great Ouse Catchment Board required extra clay banking to the three sites. The clay had to be brought from Manea, three miles away, by lorries, off-loaded onto the light railway and pushed to the site. Later the board required all the new clay to be turfed. The south bank was covered by trees and these had to be felled to create fields of fire. They were conveyed across the river and formed into a tank barrier, being wired to steel stakes. All three pillboxes were then camouflaged. Other sites around Thorney required concrete raft

This F W 3/22 pillbox at Beccles Common, clearly shows the levels of each pouring of concrete during construction. A fault has developed along that just below loophole level. TM 434908 PME.

49

At Bridgend, Glamorgan, builders were faced with the task of a two-storey pillbox, one of the unusual types they were asked to construct. ss 916794 PM36.

foundations, excavations into slopes and, in one case, a special bridge across a stream for access during construction. There were many cases where fields of fire were created involving much time and labour and it was these extras that tended to swell costs. Another extra was the necessity of building farm access bridges over the anti-tank ditches.

It was not only in Peterborough that contractors found themselves in conflict with F W 6. The Helical Bar and Engineering Co Ltd were in correspondence over the construction of five pillboxes at West Dean, near Salisbury, which had been built at the fixed rate of £1,215. The company claimed the cost had been much higher, due to having to build on wet ground on the far side of a stream. No doubt there were many more instances of similar claims, as sites must often have been chosen in June and July when the weather was fine, but later in the year were rendered unsuitable by heavy rainfall. This accounts for a number of pillboxes now water-filled and sinking in the ground.

In the west of England Mr S. G. Butland, foreman with Messrs Stansell and Sons of Taunton, remembers removing the swing bridges over the Taunton Canal and replacing them with baulks of timber for farm use. Pillboxes were built by a number of contractors, including the maintenance staff of British Cellophane, before the whole contract was placed in the hands of his firm. They completed, with sub-contractors, many hundreds of pillboxes and anti-tank defences and were responsible for their camouflage.

Mr Ted Parsons was fourteen years old in July, 1940, and left school to work for Messrs Waddingtons, civil engineers of London, who were working on the GHQ Line near Bristol. The work involved digging the anti-tank ditch and the work lasted until the spring of 1941. Ruston and Priestman excavators were used and each machine was accompanied by two labourers, whose job was to level the spoil on each side of the ditch. A 2-foot wide path was to be left on the far (enemy) side to enable the spoil bank to provide a breastwork for the infantry. One major job was the erection of prefabricated wooden bridges, made at Glastonbury, for farmers to gain access to now isolated fields. One stretch of ditch was through solid limestone, this having to be drilled and blasted, a job taking several weeks to complete.

The GHQ Line Blue was the responsibility of Messrs W. E. Chivers of Devizes, who, working along the Kennet and Avon Canal, used canal barges to ferry heavy materials to sites inaccessible by road. It was at the end of this section of the line at Theale Mill, the home of Mrs O. Hasson, that the construction of a Type 28 pillbox was photographed. At that time it was no doubt an offence under the defence regulations, but now it is the only record to survive showing the construction and reinforcement used in 1940.

Northwards from here ran GHQ Line Red, where Mr W. T. Le Sateur, the joinery manager of Messrs J. M. Jones Ltd of Maidenhead, was responsible for the construction of pillboxes in the Pangbourne-Whitchurch area. His firm was one of the subcontractors which worked under the direction of J. R. Smallbones Ltd of

Pillboxes at Hailley Farm and Walnut Tree Cottage, Warnborough

Tools required:		*Stores:*	*Materials required:*	
EXCAVATOR			Cement	×5 tons
Shovels GS	×25	Pegs, profile boards	Sand	×75 yards
Shovels SM	×5	and lines.	Aggregate-2-½in.	×140 yards
Pick Heads	×12		Steel: ¾in. bar	×700 feet or ½ton (min. length 15ft).
Helves	×12		½in. bar	×10,000 feet or 3tons (min. length 8ft).
CONCRETOR			¾in. bar	×6,000 feet or 1ton 1cwt
Bolt cutters	×2	Mixing boards and		(min. length 3ft. 9in).
Bar benders	×2	shuttering Binding	plate ½×1'6in.×1'6in.	×4
Wire cutters	×2	wire 2cwt.	plate 5'6in.×2'9in.	×2
Concrete mixers	×2		Wire 14 gauge	×½ ton
Pliers GS 7in.	×2		Batten 3×1½in.	×100ft. run.
CARPENTER			Shuttering: 4'3in.	×900ft. run.
Hand saws 26in.	×2	Nails	9×1½in.	×2,500ft.
Hammers claw 24oz	×2		2×1in.	×300ft.
Hammers claw 32oz	×2		'L' iron 1½×1½in.	×30ft.
Bolster	×2		Rag bolts ½in.	×28
Hammers club	×1		Hoop iron 1in. wide	×25 ft.
Trowels 12in.	×4		Kimolo Board 1'5in×1'0½in.×4	
Buckets GS 13in.	×6		Washers ½in. dia.	×4
Water trolley	×2		Agricultural drains 4in.	×100
Padlock 2½in with keys	×1		Gulley grids 9×9in	×2
Tool box	×1		Round steel bar ¼in. dia.	×4ft.

Streatley, the main contractors. His job was to provide the necessary formwork, prefabricated in their works, a task made difficult because of the timber shortage, as no licence was available at the time. However, the firm managed by using up short and broken scaffold boards, while other contractors used a brick skin as permanent shuttering.

Further east, along GHQ Line Blue at Bowling Alley, we are fortunate to have the notes of Mr A. C. Pinhorn, who was serving as a Garrison Engineer with the RE at Aldershot. He superintended the building of defences from west of Crondall crossroads to Farnham. Messrs J. B. Edwards Ltd and Thomas Higgs Ltd worked on these sections and were assisted by troops from the RAMC unit quartered at Queen Elizabeth Barracks. The latter not only worked on the ditch, but carried out camouflage work extremely well. The pillboxes were known at the Light Machine Gun and Medium Machine Gun type, with the larger design scheduled to receive a loophole covering flap, which opened when the weapon was brought into the firing position. These flaps were to have been delivered to South-Eastern Command, but had not arrived when Mr Pinhorn was posted abroad in 1941. Walls were reinforced with two layers of BRC fabric, while three were incorporated in the roof. Pages from Mr Pinhorn's notebook reveal the materials and tools needed to build two pillboxes at Odiham,

Hants. These were at Hailley's Farm, North Warnborough, and Walnut Tree Cottage, just across the road, and were still in existence in 1978. References on the Military Grid were Q 16827081 and Q 16747076, which are SU 728510 and SU 729511 on modern OS maps. The pillbox on the farm was built inside the timber barn, with three loopholes concealed by hinged sections of the weatherboarding. Extensions and alterations to the barn further help to hide this pillbox from view, but, inside, the concrete structure is intact. The pillbox at Walnut Tree Cottage has blended into the garden so effectively that it is invisible to the passer-by. The work on these sites was carried out by the 63 Pioneer Company and the 839 Artisan Works Company RE and it was because the pillboxes were of special construction that the calculation of tools and materials was necessary.

On the next sector of the GHQ Line Blue Mr R. H. Eggan, employed by Messrs A. H. Ball and Co Ltd of Farnham, recalled that his company built about twenty-four pillboxes in and around the town. Every fit man from the 'dole' was drafted to assist, some coming each day from Woolhampton, Berks, to work on the sites. The procedure was that the first gang excavated and put in the concrete base, then moved on to the next site. The bricklayers and carpenters arrived to build the shell and formwork for loopholes. The next gang filled the brick and wooden shuttering with concrete, being followed by the roof construction gang as soon as the walls had set firm enough. This cycle of operations was carried on until completion of the contract.

Bridgwater Bros was the main contractor for the next section of the GHQ Line to the east, but, like so many firms, kept no record of wartime activities. At Sidlow Bridge the pillboxes were built by local contractors from Reigate, Messrs G. H. Faulkner, who also built airraid shelters for local schools.

Along the GHQ Line the garrison engineers supervised the construction of pillboxes by contractors, directed military personnel allocated to dig the anti-tank ditch and were responsible for camouflage of work, both during and after construction. In addition the enclosure of company and battalion headquarters with concertina barbed wire and the clearing of fields of fire had to be supervised. The work began in May, 1940, and continued at full speed until the order to stop came in early October. Then the task of the garrison engineer was that of clearing-up, with a surplus of material and tools to collect and account for at the end of a very busy period.

At the same time as work went ahead on the GHQ Line, other contractors were working under similar conditions and pressures to complete the command and corps lines. While some of these stop-lines ran parallel to the coast, a number ran inland to prevent lateral movement of German forces which might penetrate the coastal defences. The Ringwood Stop-line in Southern Command was one of these, with 4 Division in overall charge of the siting, the infantry selecting the site and the engineers making sure the local contractors completed the job correctly.

"*Hurry up, there—we're waiting to block the road!*"

Mr R. L. Clarke, who was serving in 225 Field Company RE, recalls that his unit was responsible for the line from Fordingbridge to the coast and from Bournemouth to their headquarters at New Milton. The contractors involved were small firms which took on labour for the job. Cement was a reserved store, so an allocation was made for each site, with the price being worked on cost, plus a fixed profit. Mr Clarke, who had experience of building pillboxes in France, was not impressed by the first sites chosen around Fordingbridge. He reported this to his CRE, Colonel Coxwell-Rogers, who came down and resited them correctly. Reinforcement being in very short supply, this was omitted from the anti-tank blocks. No continuous anti-tank ditch was dug, as the River Avon was considered a sufficient barrier, but all defences were concentrated at the river crossings.

In built-up areas loopholes were cut in walls and parapets of bridges, often in support of a pillbox or strongpoint built into a shed. At the engine sheds at Salisbury a standard pre-cast loophole was built into one wall. One type of infantry 'protection' that would seem to be unique to Salisbury consisted of two parallel walls 6 feet high, 3 feet apart, without roof or ends, the wall facing the enemy having six loopholes. The exposed siting of these three fire positions on top of a railway embankment would have made them hazardous to use, a flanking enemy rifleman being able to fire a single shot straight between the walls of the three positions.

Along the coast the policy was different, with the county divisions holding a continuous line forming the 'coastal crust'. In addition to the mentioned types of defences here the minefields were an extra RE responsibility. The barbed wire defences were erected behind the beach minefields where they served two purposes: firstly, to prevent easy access from the beach by an enemy who got over the mines, and, secondly, to prevent people and animals straying into the minefields. In the first role they were never tested and in the second they were not always successful. Several members of 225 Field Company RE lost their lives to the Naval Type B Mark C mine in the area they were deployed. The sensitivity of the mine depended on the depth of sand and the strength of the operating spring, but along the coast where extra sand could be washed on top with each tide and the movement of the beach shifted mines, accidents could easily happen.

At Southampton Major Gillespie, with his 7 Field Company RE, had worked out a comprehensive defence plan, but soon after it had been implemented the supply of cement became critical and much of it was never completed. The Solent itself was protected by the Isle of Wight, which had a Chemical Warfare Company RE based there, one of the companies forming the Chemical Warfare Group at Havant under the fiery Colonel Costello. These units were responsible for the Portsmouth Garrison Defences and, as with all other special units, were engaged on defence works at this time.

The memories of an ordinary soldier who helped to construct the defences along the south coast illustrate the dangers and difficulties

The builders at Minehead made a neat job of this pillbox at the edge of the beach, with its rear-entrance stairway. SS 984464 DMS.

53

The British Army undertook much work in the construction of coastal defences, when they may have been better employed in serious training. Here they are erecting the steel scaffolding after the concrete blocks and barbed wire have been placed on the beach! [Imperial War Museum]

facing those who toiled long hours during that desperate summer. Private L. Staunton, serving with the 7th Battalion, the Wiltshire Regiment, stationed at New Milton, Hants, was one of the many soldiers whose task was to erect the scaffold anti-tank barrier. His battalion was responsible for the section of coast from Milford-on-Sea to Highcliffe. He writes, 'The scaffoldings were quite large structures, clamped together on the beach and carried bodily out into the sea by twenty-five of us, when the tide was at its lowest (often 3 or 5am in November). We used to go blue with the cold on moonlight nights and had Thermos urns of cocoa provided for us. When a long line of obstacles were carried out into the sea, all the tall men had to carry the shorter men out to join the sections together with further clamps and steel scaffolding. Sometimes the waves went right over our heads and it was indeed a very frightening experience to those of us who could not swim (sadly I couldn't). So we had to let go and jump up to gasp

54

for a breath of air.'

59 Field Company RE, based at Cowplain, undertook the defence work along the coast to Bognor Regis, which included a boom across Chichester Harbour.

The command line running from Newhaven north to Eridge was the responsibility of Mr I. S. Greeves, then employed by John Mowlem and Company, who were managing contractors for defence lines in Surrey and Sussex. This area was divided into five sections, each with its own headquarters. These were at Uckfield, Crowborough, Mayfield, Tunbridge Wells and Blindley Heath. Mr Greeves' main recollection is of having as his camouflage officer a keen amateur dramatics designer who had his own ideas on sites.

At Folkestone a local contractor, Mr O. Marx of Sandgate Road, was building the town defences, with Mr G. Leggatt in charge of the concrete mixing gang. The latter remembers that they used five tons of cement and twenty yards of ballast for each of the octagonal pillboxes, being built during a period of heavy raids during the Battle of Britain. Workmen were killed and wounded in these raids, in one instance while erecting poles to prevent a field's use by German aircraft to land troops.

A graphic account of conditions in Essex came from Mr A. B. Kennell: 'My memory of that period was one of long hours, work, poor conditions, lack of warm food in isolated parts of the country or on the beach and the dreadful tiredness we suffered without honour or glory. We were never mentioned.'

'I was on the defences of the coast; first on tide-work, erecting long iron spikes set in concrete on the beach at Jaywick. Being below the high-tide mark, what a race we had to beat the incoming tide. Working all hours of the day and night, by moonlight often enough, to finish our section, with the youngest lads fifteen years of age to one glorious old-age pensioner of eighty-two, who inspired us all with his tireless energy, working in his bare feet and legs in the cold sea water and trousers rolled above his knees.'

At that time all the residents who were able were asked to leave coastal areas, including the sick, elderly, women and children, leaving only those required to keep necessary services operating. These included water, gas, electricity, sewerage, telephones and ARP. Many of the able-bodied were either called up or left the area to work at the factories situated inland. The remainder were asked to report to the Labour Exchange and volunteer for defence work on the beaches, supplying their own tools. These included innkeepers, shop assistants and, of course, building workers. Little transport was available to get to the sites, so walking and cycling with shovels and food for a day's work was the daily routine. In addition, German aircraft were often over the coast, bombing and machine-gunning workers in exposed positions. At Pump Hill, St Osyth, one workman died following such an attack as he endeavoured to finish the top of a pillbox before the concrete set. Mr Kennell was himself under fire near a bombed farmhouse at Brightlingsea and recalls seeing three of his workmates

55

huddled flat on the ground, with a sheet of corrugated iron over them for protection, while their legs stuck out for all to see!

Mr R. Moreland, employed by Saunders and Martin of Eastbourne, remembers a German parachute mine landing on the anti-tank ditch they were digging at Allhallows October, 1940, making a large crater and flooding the work. Here the defence line consisted of a ditch behind which was barbed wire in front of a minefield. Mines were spaced at 6-foot intervals.

At Cambridge Messrs Coulson and Son were responsible for construction of defences along the River Cam between Shalford and Saffron Walden. They were instructed to build thirty-six pillboxes, but seven sites were cancelled following the change of policy. The firm also had the job of clearing and deepening the river to create an anti-tank obstacle.

In the spring of 1941 686 General Construction Company RE was posted to Hunstanton. Mr P. Connolly, then a sapper, remembers their work in Norfolk at this time. They were billeted in the empty holiday hotels and each day they set out to complete the coastal defences. These consisted of pillboxes around Heacham, associated minefields, tubular scaffolding and other anti-tank obstacles. Miles of barbed wire was erected, much being placed around airfields in the area.

Further north, Messrs A. Sinclair and Sons Ltd of Scarborough, and William Cornforth Ltd of Whitby undertook the defence work in their areas, while inland searchlight posts were nearly all built by J. Yarran and Son Ltd of Hutton Rudby.

Mr R. Hebditch, of Chas Hebditch Ltd of Loftus, found the seven-day, sixty-hour week very tiring because, due to siting pillboxes along the cliff and beach, most of the work was done by hand. At Runswick Bay and Kettleness cement, sand and ballast had to be packed in army sandbags, then carried by human chain down narrow and dangerous paths to the beaches. Water suitable for concrete was another problem, in many cases water carts having to be filled at streams, then towed or manhandled to the cliff edge, where hosepipes and buckets fed the mixing platforms. There was no shortage of material in this area and, when mechanical plant could be used, the Army produced it at once. This would have been through F W 5, the branch of the Directorate of Fortification and Works which could supply all types of heavy construction gear, including bulldozers and dumpers. Another large contractor involved in the north-east defences was Gleeson and Co Ltd.

The vast amounts of materials used nationwide, in the brief time that construction was in full swing, did lead to local shortages of some materials, especially steel reinforcement. During post-war demolition of a pillbox at Brookwood, Surrey, the reinforcement used was found to be park railings, no doubt removed during the drive for scrap metal.

Inspection of a crumbling pillbox at Middle Wallop, Hants, showed that bedsprings were the main reinforcement and Brigadier

" Private property, I suppose"

H. E. Hopthrow revealed in *The Royal Engineers Journal* that one of the principal suppliers was 'Slumberland'.

After the initial phase of construction by the contractors was over, the Royal Engineers were kept busy through the early part of 1941 strengthening and repairing defences along the coast, some of which suffered damage in the winter gales. Mr E. Roberts, second-in-command of 725 Construction Company RE from February to July, 1941, noted that, having just been reformed from 725 Bomb Disposal Company, they moved from London to Folkestone. The unit was engaged on beach defences from east of Folkestone to Hythe waterfront. The 'gap' blown in Folkestone Pier was widened to fifty yards and concrete 'pimples' were built through the town almost to the *Valiant Sailor*. With nineteen concrete mixers hired from local builders, the output was as high as 100 per day. One unusual pillbox was hung from the underside of the pier over the beach. Loopholes faced east and west, while entry was through a cast-iron manhole in the pier deck.

Finally a word must be said about the extensive schemes for flooding water meadows, making them impassable for vehicles. At Castle Eaton, near Swindon, a system of flooding the meadows along the River Thames was created in 1940. The remains of a sluice were used in 1975 by Messrs Blatcon Ltd as the bank seats for a new pre-stressed concrete bridge. On the River Wylye, north-west of Salisbury, 100 small dams were called for to raise water levels enough to create a tank barrier. These were to be 3 feet 6 inches above the river bed, using a tree trunk as the base. With 4-inch posts as anchors, rabbit wire held together the chalk filling. In addition fourteen excavators dredged the river between Salisbury and Bishopstrow, near Warminster. All this work was not appreciated by local residents, who complained bitterly about changed water levels downstream. Mr J. Sutton of Stoford claimed £50 damages, as he had no fishing or water for his vegetable garden! No doubt other schemes involving rivers and canals had their problems, but by the middle of 1941 most work had ceased and very little remains of this type of defence.

As will be realized the defence of Britain in 1940 was a nationwide effort by the Army and civilian building contractors. Involving large quantities of materials, often on difficult sites, under wartime conditions and at great speed, it reflects tremendous credit to a little-publicized industry.

CHAPTER SEVEN

Camouflage of Defences

A shed built onto the end of a house, in matching materials, could conceal a pillbox, such as this one at Acle, Norfolk. TG 402105 DMSE.

THE TACTICAL USE OF the pillbox relied on it being hidden from sight until the enemy were within effective range of its weapons. The problem of camouflage was approached in two ways: firstly by disguising the pillbox as another type of building, and, secondly, by painting it in a disruptive pattern, usually green and brown, to merge into the landscape.

In the first instance, some were built within barns and similar buildings, while others adjoined buildings, being camouflaged as lean-to sheds. The defence lines did not always provide sites with such an easy answer to concealment and much ingenuity was used in the many and varied disguises employed. Mr S. G. Butland, working on the Taunton Stop-line, remembers Oliver Messel, the theatrical scenic designer, accompanying him on a tour of sites. At each he made a sketch of the camouflage to be used to blend with the immediate surroundings – a number to look like hay or straw stacks, while some along the canal resembled workmen's huts. At Ilminster railway station one, partly sunk into an embankment, was covered with coal and, by the addition of wheelbarrow and shovel, made to appear part of the coalyard. In Ilton village a pillbox was completed as a bus shelter, with clock-face and timetables on the walls. Occasionally ideas became rather grand, as in the case of Dillington Park. The job started with plenty of material, but the efforts to build a mini-castle soon used these, with the result that local timber was cut to make the imitation stone wall panels. These were frames holding reinforcement, covered with concrete, marked to look like stone. They were costly of both time and materials, so Oliver Messel obtained imitation stone, made of plaster on canvas, from Elstree Studios. The pillbox was thus quickly completed, with battlements, to match the lodge gatehouse. At this time Sapper Ronald Searle, 287 Field Company RE, was at work in Norfolk.

A more simple way to make screens was by using a framework of fire poles, covered with wire netting onto which had been sprayed paint and chicken feathers. This was widely used as camouflage and for a number of years after the war this type of wire netting could be seen in use around chicken houses, fulfilling its original purpose. In fact in September, 1944, an Army Order stated that wire netting from pillboxes could be salvaged for use as chicken runs etc. Papier-mâché

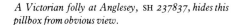

This Folkestone garage, TR *241379, was rather given away by it's hexagonal shape, but the petrol pump added the extra touch of authenticity.* [Kent Messenger]

screens, painted to resemble cottages, walls and roof tiles were used, but after a year in the British climate had badly deteriorated. By then, however, the threat of invasion was past.

Folkestone had its share of camouflaged pillboxes, with examples of bathing cubicles along the front and a fine public convenience on the path from the harbour to the cliff top. The latter, complete with the usual two screened entrances, had the loopholes covered with dummy windows. The unit signwriter of 725 Construction Company RE, neatly lettered 'Ladies' and 'Gentlemen' on the entrances, finally completing his work with the large notice 'Public Conveniences'. When he had finished, he summed up his thoughts with the words 'If the . . . can't read English – I'm wasting my time'.

The natural setting of Pevensey Castle helped to camouflage this pillbox at TQ 645047.

This garden shed at Aylsham, Norfolk, TG 197275, was in reality a pillbox covering the crossing of the River Bure. The wood and corrugated-iron roof were fixed to the concrete, remaining until recent years as a good example of camouflage.

Nearby, at this time, Mr G. Legatt, having completed the pillboxes in Folkestone, was working on the dummy guns – telegraph poles pointing out to sea – watched by Winston Churchill, who was making an inspection of defences in the south-east.

Inland, at Tonbridge, a large sign inviting the visitor to the attractions of Castle Gardens hid one pillbox from view. At seaside resorts kiosks and bookstalls were popular forms of camouflage. One, sited at Brighton's Preston Circus, was lettered P. C. Brown, Newsagent, while another, on the beach below the Fayrness Hotel, Margate, was labelled as a W. H. Smith bookstall. Here and there a sense of humour prevailed over the grim situation, with a Worthing kiosk (T Q 149025) being under the ownership of 'Hyam Ready'. At Eastbourne a canvas screen painted to resemble an old Roman Wall (T Q 591465) by local builder, Mr Martin, to hide a pillbox, bore a plaque with the inscription that it was built by Martinus Maximus. The same kind of humour led to a pillbox at Ipswich being painted 'A. Mole, Tunnel Contractor, Deepdownham, Suffolk', and another at Woodbridge bearing an advertising hoarding for the 'Hotel Continental – Warm reception for visiting troops'.

Along the roads petrol stations, complete with pumps, sprang up, but would never serve the motorist the Pool Petrol advertised. One of this type was at Newlands Corner, Surrey, where, in addition, a number of pillboxes were disguised as roadside cafés, a feature of prewar Britain. Mrs Edna Beale well remembers the similarly camouflaged pillbox at Norris Bridge, Pyestock (S U 833536), because, as a child, she and her friends allowed a visiting aunt to take their 'orders' for ice cream as they approached the 'café'. This style of camouflage was widespread and, as late as 1975, the words 'Teas', 'Tizer', 'Café' and 'Snacks' were just readable on a pillbox at Blindley Heath, Surrey (T Q 364452). They must have used good paint.

The quality of paint is confirmed by a site at Bournemouth (S Z 089925). Camouflaged as a summerhouse, with painted windows and topped with pyramidal roof, thousands of people passed it without a second thought as to its true purpose. It was only when the roof was removed and the concrete hexagon covered with posters that it became an eyesore. This was one site that should have been preserved.

At Wragby, Lincolnshire, a rectangular pillbox (T F 133780) in the Market Place was built as a bus shelter. On the second storey provision was made for a Bren gun on an anti-aircraft mount, surrounded by a crenellated parapet. It became known as Bateman's Folly, after Sergeant A. Bateman who was responsible for its construction.

Pillboxes were disguised as railway waggons, dockside cranes, roundabouts, car park attendants' huts and even motor vans. The effort to create just one scheme can be judged by the account of Mr A. C. Pinhorn, when he turned a hexagonal mass of concrete into a sports pavilion: 'The slabwood covering was obtained from the RE Roads and Forest Depot, Aldershot, where trees were trimmed after felling.

Roadside garages were often convenient places to locate pillboxes at the entrance to a town or village. Fordingbridge, Hampshire, was no exception, the close-up reveals the loopholes in the wall. SU 151142 DMS (demolished).

The scantlings were used in the construction of barracks, whilst the outer cut, complete with bark, was waste. This, with the bark showing on the outside, was used to make screens for pillboxes, making them look like the timber buildings often found in the countryside. The framework forming the basis of the screens was made from saplings, cut either in clearing the site or field of fire. The old steel casement windows came from the salvage depot at Tongham and the uralite sheets from scrap left from roofing the local barracks. The football field did not exist before the pillbox. This was marked out properly and goal posts erected by the local RAMC boys, who had been given the morning off to give it the appearance of having been used a lot!'

Camouflage by concealment was achieved by breaking up the outline by using pattern and colour, a technique originated in modern warfare by a group of young French artillerymen in the First World War. Painters in civilian life, and on the receiving end of German artillery fire, they applied their knowledge of tone and colour to the problem of concealment. Objects are first recognized by their form, tone and finally colour. The first thing is to break up the form and to do this it is necessary to disrupt the normal shading and shadows. These must be altered to prevent an observer from seeing a recognizable object from his viewpoint.

As an object may be viewed from several points, different aspects will need a different approach to camouflage. From the air hard shadows need concealing as they can reveal true purpose despite disruptive patterns. On the ground the vertical outline is important and should not break unnaturally into the skyline. Pillboxes, being generally symmetrical in shape, need their outlines broken, which can be accomplished by using netting with earth piled against the walls or even on the roof. Loopholes can be covered with painted scrim to

A 'mini-castle' in Wales would be a fair description of this pillbox at Trearddur Bay, Anglesey. SH 256793 CMSE.

61

match the disruptive pattern. Where sites were exposed, bold patterns were painted on the walls, the normal colours being green and brown.

Notes on camouflage, supplied to Mr Hugh Cave of Peterborough, were as follows: 'Pillboxes situated in *cornfields* will only have the *roofs* painted provided the shuttering is of brick. When the corn is cut and the field ploughed, additional treatment will be necessary. Pillboxes situated on banks or permanent grassland will have *roof and walls* painted.

'The main principles in painting are:–

1. Vertical walls should be painted diagonally rather than directly vertically.
2. Design should be flowing and not stop on the edge or corner. In cases where roofs only are being painted, the camouflage must extend to the brickwork.
3. The design must be bold and irregular.
4. The darker tone must be utilised to include the loopholes.
5. Difference in tone is as essential as difference in colour.'

Sketches from Norfolk — another page shows a milk bar, a clump of bushes and a holiday chalet. These sketches, made in July 1943, show the pillboxes before weather and time destroyed the illusions.

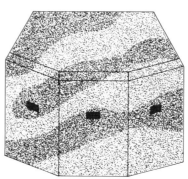

Camouflage painting.
left:
1. Slots in darker tone
2. Pattern flowing — no breaks in design
3. Pattern as near horizontal as possible.

right: WRONG
1. Slots in light tone
2. Breaks in design
3. Pattern too vertical

This pillbox used a 'for sale' notice, with apt wording, as it's sole effort at camouflage at Hitchin, Hertfordshire. TL 193298 PM36. The wartime picture also shows the small table painted with gas detector paint. [Hitchin Museum]

The notes were accompanied by the sketches reproduced.

There was plenty of advice in publications aimed at the Home Guard market about camouflage of pillboxes. Norman Demuth, in his book *Harrying the Hun,* said: 'In the first place, it does not mean sloshing paint about willy-nilly. It means taking a concrete block and making it disappear (melt) into the countryside. It does not mean making that block look like something it is not. It may be terribly funny to come across 'Ladies' and 'Gentlemen' written on a building in the middle of a heath, or a shop on a roundabout in the centre of a town. Camouflage is intended to conceal not reveal.'

While much was done either to disguise or camouflage pillboxes, little could be done to hide the rows of anti-tank obstacles or ditches. From the air these must have always shown up, giving away general

Left: This fine example of a camouflaged pillbox survived in original condition until recent years, when the roof was removed and it became subject to fly-posting. It covers an important road junction over a railway tunnel out of Bournemouth, Dorset. SZ 089925 PCW.

Below left: A view from the other side reveals the truth about the summerhouse. SZ 089925.

Below: Close-up the detail of the camouflage paintwork can clearly be seen.

defence lines to the enemy.

Last but not least important was the hiding of the tracks to sites both during and after construction from aerial reconnaissance. Contractors were shown aerial photos of their sites in an endeavour to make them camouflage-conscious. Light-coloured spoil heaps were sprayed with green paint, vehicle tracks re-routed to match gateways and barbed wire sited so that each pillbox was *not* surrounded by a neat circle of grass that cattle could not reach.

The Home Guard Fieldcraft Manual, commenting on the revealing air photo of a pillbox under construction, said; 'Doubtless the shine of the pillbox will later be camouflaged, possibly the spoil in the field and tracks will be ploughed under, but what is the good of doing all this long after the vital information has been given already? Camouflage is not something to be added at a later date, it is a discipline to be kept from the moment you begin to construct war-like works.'

The other constructions which came under the heading of camouflage were the dummy pillboxes of which 200 were sited in

The Dairy House at Beaulieu, Hampshire, with its attractive hexagonal roof, conceals a concrete pillbox with loopholes to cover the adjacent river. SU 388023 DMW.

Work in progress on defence construction of pillboxes and the anti-tank ditch at Crondall, Hampshire. SU 8034495. The wheeltracks leading to the various sites can clearly be seen, showing up in a lighter shade.

Eastern Command, with 100 each in 43 Div and 44 Div areas. Also in 43 Div area there were other dummy defences including two 15-inch guns, two 9.9 railway guns, twelve field battery sites and many trenches. In the event, shortage of materials and labour restricted the numbers erected. It was found that the dummies were almost as expensive as the real thing and, with the change of tactics, there were plenty of real pillboxes to act as decoys to attract fire. One at Eastbourne was purpose-built to draw enemy fire, being nothing more than a solid chunk of concrete with dummy loopholes.

At this time camouflage of tents was under review, when it was found that a disruptive pattern made them more obvious. The final solution was that 60% of tents were to be Standard Colour No. 1A and 40% to be colour No. 7.

CHAPTER EIGHT

Pillbox Tactics

THE CHANGING STRATEGY OF defence policies has been discussed in Chapter 2, but the tactical use of the pillboxes also deserves consideration.

Tactical Notes for Platoon Commanders, 1941 had this to say about 'A Post in Concrete'. It is interesting to note that in some official instructions the term 'pillbox' was only applied to those of the circular type F W 3/25, the rest being described as 'strong posts'.

'1 The concrete pillbox is a great aid to defence if intelligently used; if not, it may become a death-trap.

2 Concrete is a protection against bullets, shell splinters and weather. Sometimes it affords protection against shell fire. If properly camouflaged it is also a protection from ground and air observation.

3 Many concrete posts are not complete protection against a direct hit from a shell or aerial bomb. They all have the disadvantage of limiting the field of view and the field of fire. The garrison will be unable to use all their rifles at one and the same time because of the fewness of the loopholes. Finally the garrison is hindered in the employment of the hand grenade and bayonet.'

Guidelines were given as to the manner in which sentries on duty outside the post should be able to see and hear all around them. Temporary cover could be taken during shell fire and bombing, but a watch for enemy approaching under these conditions should be vigilant. The light machine-gun should fire from the pillbox, if it can carry out the alloted task, during an attack, but men who cannot use weapons inside must man trenches outside. If the pillbox was surrounded, except for those who could fire from a loophole, the garrison would fight outside where they could employ all their weapons to the best advantage.

The notes, prepared in February, 1941, and amended in March, 1941, illustrate the official army view, which, with other references, are summarized as follows:

Firstly, pillboxes were part of a whole defence scheme, which provided them with supporting fire trenches to prevent infiltration by the enemy. This infantry support meant keeping the enemy at a distance from which they could not effectively use close-range

Sited on the side of the cliff, this pillbox covered the beach at Lulworth Cove, Dorset, providing some cover for the men in an open situation. SY 825797 CCNE.

65

Loopholes in walls gave extra fire points for defenders. These were at Salisbury, on the then south-western approaches of the city. SU 129304 L/H.

weapons such as flame-throwers and grenades.

Secondly, pillboxes often had barbed-wire perimeters and mines would have been laid to prevent an easy approach by enemy troops. Mines were to have been used in some numbers: the records show that 13,500 would have been laid at selected sites along the GHQ Line between Maiden Bradley and West Dean, a distance of forty-four miles.

Finally, if enemy forces got within grenade or flame-thrower range the pillbox was to be evacuated. Thus it will be seen that the pillbox, properly sited and equipped with weapons, was an effective part of the 1940 defences, filling the gap in our armoury caused by the lack of tanks.

In addition to being sited along defence lines, pillboxes were built at defensive strong points: 'Nodal Points', 'Islands' or 'Anti-tank Islands', to use terms fashionable in the 1940s. It was recommended that they be built with loopholes about 18 inches above the ground, to give the best trajectory for machine-gun fire and give a lower profile to the enemy. Wherever possible two or three pillboxes were to be sited to give mutual fire support, the effectiveness of the defences then being greatly increased. In most cases infantry support trenches, or section posts, were built to hold a section of ten men in the vicinity. At Fordingbridge, Hants, these were of a substantial nature, with concrete roofs. Still surviving in 1984, they are brick and concrete structures with ten loopholes at or near ground level. They are 'V' or 'L' shaped in plan and flank pillboxes that defend this nodal point, an important crossing of the River Avon.

The Home Guard training manuals and similar publications

Downright dangerous could be the description of these infantry fire positions along the railway at Salisbury. SU 153133.

stressed that, although pillboxes and road blocks had their uses, they must not make the Home Guard 'village Maginot-minded'. It was not just a case of sitting in a pillbox and shooting straight. Where they were available they should be used, but they were not a substitute for good fieldcraft and weapon training. They were considered as 'static armour', needing, just as tanks, full infantry and artillery support to be really effective. The larger pillboxes could emplace the 2-pounder gun, in 1940 the standard tank weapon. The smaller types with their machine-guns would equate with the light tank of the period.

Pillboxes correctly sited and constructed, equipped with the right weapons, were the nearest equivalent to a tank hull-down that could be built in quantity in the short time available. It is significant to recall that, later in the war, tanks, dug-in in a hull-down position, were commonly used as pillboxes, often holding up advances by the allies. Pillboxes were themselves used by the German and Japanese armies, while bunkers dug into the ground added to the Allies' difficulties. Prior to crossing the River Rhine in 1944, pillboxes were labouriously 'taken-out' by artillery, one at a time. The American gunners found they could destroy them with three rounds of 155mm gunfire, while remaining out of range of small arms fire. The 9th USAAF History mentions pillboxes as specific targets for Thunderbolts of 366th Squadron around St Lo on 11 July, 1944. In 1940 the destruction of pillboxes by a German invasion force would have taken up much artillery fire where infantry could not clear the way. This would have taken time and quantities of ammunition which would have been shipped across the English Channel. Thus pillboxes would have contributed to the logistic problems of the invader. The British defence plan was that of fighting a holding action until a counter-attack could be mounted by mobile forces and in this role the pillbox would have served its purpose.

Here it is appropriate to recall the memories of those who actually manned pillboxes in earnest. Peter Griffiths was in one of the small units defending the Suffolk coast, doing '24 hours on' and '24 hours off' as the normal duty. The '24 on' being in the pillbox, chilly in November, and the '24 off' under canvas, equally chilly. Duty in the pillbox meant sand in food and everything else, but during the '24 off' it was a trip to Lowestoft that was a treat, unless the siren sounded, then it was back to camp and to the pillbox. Armed with a Vickers .303, orders were that every round had to be fired at the enemy, then dismantle the gun and use the pieces in hand-to-hand fighting! Molotov Cocktails were supplied and the area in front was mined, but the anti-tank blocks were badly damaged in the winter storms of 1940. Forty years on, Peter still remembers cleaning his metal dinner plate in the fine sand after each meal.

Along the south coast three pillboxes were commanded by Henry Manning, who found his original notes of the Brigade Commander's inspection on 22 October, 1941. General Comments concerned: road blocks – men should be told off and trained to close them quickly; gaps in tubular scaffold should be closed more quickly with men

A strongly defended crossing of the Kennet and Avon Canal near Hampstead Marshall, Berkshire.
SU 424671 PMS.

An infantry section post in concrete at Fordingbridge, Hampshire, one of a number defending this important 'anti-tank island' and crossing point on the River Avon.
SU 144137 LMS.

The combination of anti-tank blocks and pillbox, camouflaged as a railway yard shed, are well shown in this picture of Wimborne Station. All have now been demolished. SZ 018997 PCN and A/TB.

The view of a defender of High Post airfield would have got from his pillbox at Great Durnford. Nothing could have gone past without his knowing. SU 138373 PCW.

The interior fittings of the larger pillboxes included a shelf to each loophole, which could be folded down when not needed. These were usually taken for firewood and are not often seen in surviving emplacements. The steel shutter which restricts the size of the loophole is raised by pulling the chain above the aperture, and fixing it to the hook. SZ 294933 DMS.

Special pillboxes for special places: this mini-pillbox is situated to meet a threat from the north for Marlborough, Wiltshire. SU 189693 DCN.

needing more training; hessian screens must be correctly sited and hung; ammunition, especially in pillboxes, to be cleaned and inspected regularly; range cards to be made for Bren and mortar teams; post commanders to check all stores in post and pillboxes, such as light signals, ammunition, food and water. Pillboxes were to have a reserve of water and three days' hard rations. The pillboxes bore the names Hellfaya Corner, Snackers and Gull's Nest.

Hellfaya Corner	*Snackers*	*Gull's Nest*
Platoon Commander	Section Corporal	Platoon Sergeant
Section Corporal		Section Corporal
7 men	6 men	6 men
1 × 6pdr gun + 48 rounds	1 LMG + 2,000 rounds	1 MMG + 5,000 rounds
1 MMG + 5,000 rounds	1 A/T Rifle	1 LMG + 2,000 rounds
1 LMG + 2,000 rounds	1 searchlight	1 × 2 in. mortar
Verey Pistol	Water + rations	Water + rations
Water + rations	1 cook	
	1 driver	

Later, as the Home Guard became more efficient and better equipped, concrete went out of fashion and the pillboxes were used as targets for the new weapons. Mr G. Thornally, of Worlington, Suffolk, remembers that one was used by the Cambs/Suffolk Battalion HG as the target for a spigot mortar attack. 'I would think that 5–10 rounds were fired by the spigot mortar. Looking back on my tank experience, I doubt if anyone would have survived after the first hit. I do not recollect any misses. An effective tool. The pillbox, however, would still be usable for a new lot of occupants! 'The range was 600/700 yards.

Another method of destruction was practised at the battle course attended by Mr B. H. Hall, who served with 2010 Transport Company of the Suffolk Home Guard: 'We were told that pillboxes were traps and would never be used, but it was possible that a small party of Germans could hide out in them. Our job was to flush them out. The method was one company under the OC, divided into three squads. Two to surround the box and give covering fire. The third squad to place charges, after blowing a path through the barbed wire with a Bangalore Torpedo. This was a long steel pipe, at least 2 inches in diameter, filled with explosive, the ends sealed and completed with an 8-second fuse. Slid under the wire and exploded, it cut the barbed wire into hundreds of small pieces and a path was made. This party retired, whilst another three men advanced under heavy covering fire with an explosive charge. One held the pole with a half-box at the end, something like a builder's hod, which held a slab of gun cotton and an 8/10-second fuse. This he propped against the side of the pillbox, leaving them a few seconds to dash for cover. I have seen a pillbox just lift off the ground and break into pieces.' This training was undertaken at the 54th Divisional Battle School at Aldeburgh and

The ideal site for setting an anti-tank barrier. This is a narrow road between two very steep banks at East Dean, Hampshire where, until recent years, the steel rails remained already, as they had done since 1940.
SU 281267 A/TR.

accounts for, at the least, the destruction of one along the Saxmund-ham–Ipswich railway line. This method does not take into account supporting fire from an enemy in the vicinity of the pillbox and destruction under these circumstances would have been a hazardous matter. No doubt the occupants would also have taken part in their own defence. The very fact that all through the war pillboxes and bunkers were considered necessary for defence, and were equally considered as vital targets for attackers, confirms they had a place in the tactical scheme of things in 1940. Along the GHQ Line pillboxes provided the emplacements for 2-pounder anti-tank guns at points where it was thought likely that enemy tanks could be expected, while the Vickers machine-guns and Bren guns could provide crossfire covering long stretches of the Kennet and Avon Canal, which served as the anti-tank barrier. This pattern of defence was repeated over some hundreds of miles of inland defences and a similar pattern existed around the coast.

A spigot mortar base covers an important road junction at Southampton. The steel pintle is the give-away on top of the concrete cylinder. The mortars, also known as the Blacker Bombard, provided the Home Guard with an anti-tank capability. The bases are the sole concrete reminders of this fine wartime organisation.
SU 441161 SMB.

Conclusions

"It looks to me like one of last season's machine-gun nests"

PROPERLY ARMED, CONSTRUCTED AND sited, pillboxes proved to be tough obstacles to attacking forces throughout the Second World War. They often required artillery fire or air attack for their destruction. The extra shells and bombs needed added to logistic problems and, by taking effective firepower from places where it could have been more useful, weakened the attacking potential of the attacker. Casualties in assaulting concrete defences were higher in men and materials, thus imposing a higher cost for each advance. The extra protection kept defenders' casualties lower and raised morale. Having made the point, it must be qualified by saying that the disadvantage of the pillbox is that, being static, the battle has to be fought where it was built. The arrival of the tank on the battle scene in the First World War brought the movable pillbox into warfare. In the Second World War an armoured vehicle built on a tracked tractor chassis in New Zealand because of the tank shortage was named the 'mobile pillbox', the same principle as the 'armadillos' and 'bisons' built on lorry chassis in Britain in 1940.

It is fashionable now to laugh at pillboxes and the Maginot Line concept, but in the 1960s the United States Minutemen missiles were buried deep in concrete and in the 1980s concrete shelters are still being built for the protection of aircraft on the ground. What was so funny about providing concrete to protect men in 1940?

It is easy to decry recent history, but events did not test the 1940 defences, as, even in France, the German Army elected to by-pass the Maginot Line. The Battle of Britain decided the control of the air over the Germans' selected invasion area in Britain's favour and the German war machine turned its attention to Russia. There is no doubt that the people of Britain would have fought from every beach, town, village, city and pillbox, with that unique 1940 spirit that could have bled the German Army to death.

> 'Hitler has taken Poland.
> Hitler has taken Denmark and Norway.
> Hitler has taken Holland, Belgium and France,
> He will not take this pillbox!'
>
> J. Smith, Corporal,
> Home Guard.

70

A summary of defences in Scottish Command – SCOTCO

Lt-Col A. F. Toogood, Senior Staff Officer RE for Operations and Training at the Headquarters.

'To GET A GOOD picture of the defence situation in SCOTCO at the time of Dunkirk, I have to rely on memory. I kept no diary and in everything I say this must be borne in mind.

'In strength the command averaged three or four active divisions, including the Poles. Only about 80% of the fighting arms had rifles. Reserves of small arms ammunition were incredibly small, about 60 rounds per man. Nearly all the two dozen field guns were 75mm weapons and the two or three 25-pdrs were without sights, having to be fired along the barrel line. Ammunition was short. The eight anti-tank guns were allotted to the training establishment. Coast defence artillery was relatively better, as most beaches were covered by three guns, from 6-inch downwards.

'We had no intelligence of our own country i.e. no information on likely defence lines. Reliance was placed on the Ordnance Survey and Bartholomew maps for topographical features, in particular river lines. This was necessary for bridge demolition. Beyond this our practical knowledge of the countryside was nil.

'From the above it can be seen that we were incapable of fighting a battle after Dunkirk, because of this lack of equipment and ammunition. I think that Orkney and Shetland garrisons were adequately prepared at this time. However, SCOTCO were not seriously worried by attempts at invasion, unless of course the naval and air situation deteriorated badly.

'Our immediate anti-invasion tasks (by General Staff and RE) were for commanders to choose and develop possible defensive positions. These to include beaches, inland sites and focal points; in addition, units and training formations were reformed to meet the new threat.

'The principal task for the Royal Engineers, with the co-operation of other units, was to initiate defence works, which, in the main were:

  Airfield protection against land attack.
  Collection of RE Intelligence. Information for demolitions.
  Construction of Defences – mainly pillboxes and anti-tank obstacles.

Distribution of Engineer Stores – barbed wire, explosives, land mines and anti-aircraft landing poles.

'Within a short space of time, pillboxes were sprouting all over Scotland, built mainly by contractors (through our RE Works Services) whilst the concrete anti-tank obstacles created numerous road blocks. In mountainous districts, arrangements were made to crater roads; here the geography of the land made them effective.

'One day my Colonel and I, accompanied by a General Staff Officer, were ordered to make a recce for the last line of defence for Great Britain, similar, it would seem, to Hitler's last line in the Bavarian Alps towards the end of the war. The recce took us a whole day and night, less two hours sleep in the only hours of darkness at this latitude. Our chief trouble was the unwitting obstruction by the Local Defence Volunteers (Home Guard) looking out for the mythical "Fifth Columnists" – to be seriously considered if a similar occasion arises again.'

The chosen line went through Fife, from Kirkcaldy – over the high Lomond Hills–Newburgh–Perth–Dunkeld–Schiehallion Mountain–Rannoch Moor–to the sea at Glencoe.

'It will be seen that this line depended on the mountains as an anti-tank obstacle, as we had no tanks or anti-tank guns for the area. Across to Fife, we ordered every mechanical digger in Scotland; luckily nearly all were located in the Glasgow area. I think about 170 diggers were used to dig the 20–30 mile continuous anti-tank ditch across the Fife Plain. Apart from being a "keep", SCOTCO thought Fife our most vulnerable area, as, with miles of beaches on the east coast, it was considered a landing could be made here. The Firths of Forth and Tay could have provided protection on the flanks of an attack by the Germans, who would then have been free to thrust towards Edinburgh or Glasgow. For this reason the major resources of the army were concentrated here by the fighting troops and RE's.

'Although a Sapper Officer, by implication I should have faith in defence works; most of the work done in my opinion was a waste of time, except as a morale booster: "Something must and *is* being done." In particular the pillboxes were "death-traps". Mostly built of thin brickwork, they were obvious targets and too weak to keep out concentrated small arms fire. Their only likely use would be to attract enemy fire from other defences. My view is that mobility is the only form of defence with weak forces. Unless this principle is accepted, the Maginot mentality soon affects morale.

'Concealed field defences are of great value provided that their construction does not interfere with the training of troops in the battlefield role. The road blocks would have been useful provided they were well covered by direct fire from defending troops. Airfields and a few focal points of defence would have static defences; our issues of barbed wire would have been of great use, if used properly by the RAF. There was no shortage of this material. The RAF might have suffered terribly by their lack of Field Military Engineers. At our level we took over the laid-down responsibilities for the provision of main defence stores, in particular barbed wire. This was issued to the 60–70 airfields in the command. We carried out the work of erecting poles against aircraft landings around airfields and other open spaces.

'Morale was good in SCOTCO, but there was a dangerous note of pessimism in the belief that the Germans had about 300 divisions, whereas we only acknowledged having fifty or so. This difference, due to a misuse of statistics, was due to basic differences between the British and German Armies. I knew at the time that we had mobilized much more thoroughly than the enemy. Converting the British and German organizations to a common denominator, we had in Scotland the equivalent of twelve or more German divisions, against the three/four we acknowledged. At a national level this would have given us an equivalent of 200 divisions to meet the 300 German divisions.

'By early October we in the army breathed again, for by that time we had the ammunition and equipment to defeat any invasion. Defeat was only then possible in the long term if we lost command of the sea, not forgetting air power in this context.

'To summarise; in my view the time spent by fighting troops, especially REs, in making doubtful permanent defence works would have been better spent in advanced training. On the other hand, obstacles such as anti-tank blocks and ditches were worthwhile if effectively covered by fire. Demolition arrangements for bridges, railways and oil stores were essential. Concealed field defences on a few selected lines should be carried out, if troop training is not neglected.

'I write the above, as I do not agree with Henry Ford's dictum. "History is Bunk", and that any history of events in 1940 should bring out lessons learnt at that time.'

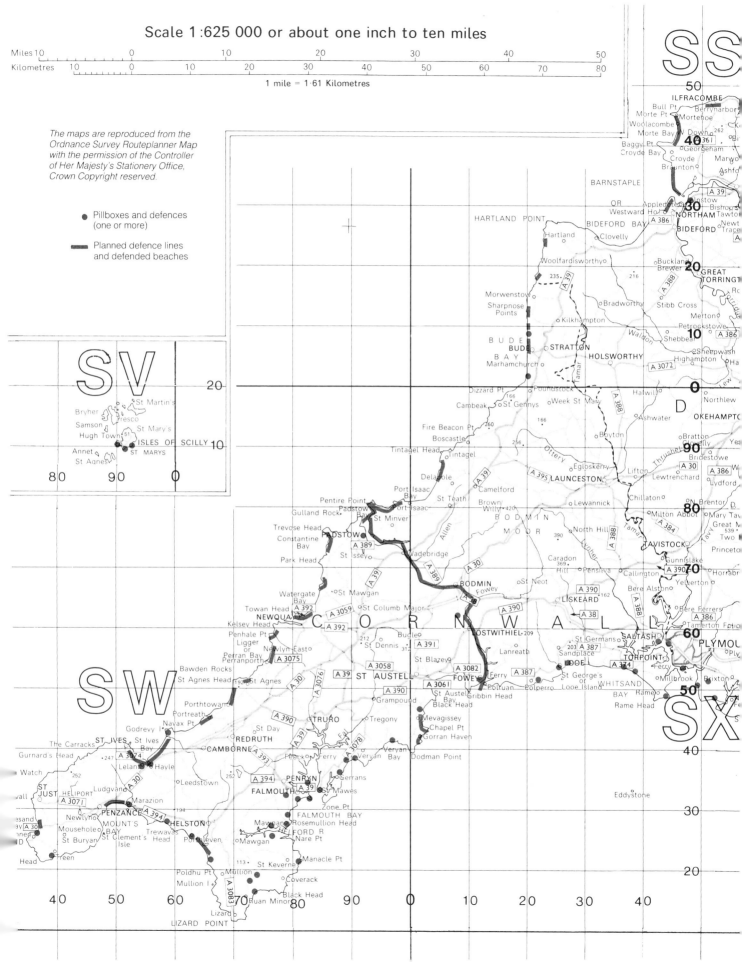

Scale 1:625 000 or about one inch to ten miles

Miles 10 ... 0 ... 10 ... 20 ... 30 ... 40 ... 50

Kilometres 10 ... 0 ... 10 ... 20 ... 30 ... 40 ... 50 ... 60 ... 70 ... 80

1 mile = 1·61 Kilometres

The maps are reproduced from the Ordnance Survey Routeplanner Map with the permission of the Controller of Her Majesty's Stationery Office, Crown Copyright reserved.

● Pillboxes and defences (one or more)

▬ Planned defence lines and defended beaches

SS

50

40

30

20

10

0

90

80

70

60

50

SX

40

30

20

SV

20

10

80 90 0

SW

40 50 60 70 80 90 0 10 20 30 40

ILFRACOMBE
Bull Pt Berrynarbor
Morte Pt Mortehoe
Woolacombe W Down 262
Morte Bay 361
Baggy Pt Georgeham
Croyde Marywo
Croyde Bay Braunton Ashfo

BARNSTAPLE

OR Instow
Westward Ho! Appledore Bishop's NORTHAM Tawto
HARTLAND POINT A 386 BIDEFORD Newt
Hartland A 39 Trace A
BIDEFORD BAY Clovelly Buckland
Woolfardisworthy Brewer GREAT TORRINGT
235. A 39 216 Stibb Cross Merton Ro
Morwenstow Bradworthy Petrockstowe A 386
Sharpnose Kilkhampton Waldon Shebbear Highampton A 386
Points Sheepwash Ha
B U D E HOLSWORTHY Highampton
BUDE STRATTON A 3072
BAY Marhamchurch Tamar 0
Dizzard Pt Poundstock Halwill Northlew
Cambeak St Gennys 166 Week St Mary A 388 Ashwater OKEHAMPTO
Fire Beacon Pt 260 166 Boyton D
Boscastle 256 Ottery Bratton
Tintagel Head Tintagel Egloskerry Lifton Thrushel Lewtrenchard Lydford W
Delabole A 39 Camelford A 395 LAUNCESTON A 30 A 386
Port Isaac St Teath Chillaton N Brentor
Bay Brown Milton Abbot Mary Tav D
Pentire Point Port Isaac Willy 420 B O D M I N North Hill A 384 Great M
Padstow St Minver M O O R 390 Tamar 539 Two
Gulland Rock Allen Caradon TAVISTOCK Princeto
Trevose Head PADSTOW 369 Penstva Gunnislake
Constantine A 389 Wadebridge A 389 Hill Callington A 390 Horrabr
Bay St Issey A 30 BODMIN St Neot LISKEARD Bere Alston Yelverton
Park Head Fowey 162 A 390 Bere Ferrers A 386
Watergate A 39 A 390 A 38 Tamerton Folio
Bay St Mawgan A 3059 St Columb Major LOSTWITHIEL 209 St Germans SALTASH 60 PLYMOU
Towan Head A 392 A 38 St Germans A 387 TORPOINT PLY
NEWQUAY C O R N W A L L Bucle 212 St Dennis 312 A 391 Lanreath Sandplace A 374 Ferry Millbrook Brixton
Kelsey Head A 392 St Blazey A 3058 A 387 LOOE WHITSAND
Penhale Pt Ligger A 3075 ST AUSTELL A 3082 Ferry A 387 St George's BAY Rame
or Newlyn East A 3016 A 390 FOWEY Polruan Polperro Looe Island Rame Head
Perran Bay A 3061 St Austell Gribbin Head 50
Perranporth Grampound Bay Black Head
Bawden Rocks St Agnes A 30 Mevagissey
St Agnes Head St Day Chapel Pt
Porthtowan A 390 TRURO Tregony Gorran Haven
Portreath Navax Pt REDRUTH A 39 Veryan
Godrevy I St Ives CAMBORNE A 393 Feock Ferry Veryan Dodman Point
The Carracks ST IVES Lelant A 3074 Gerrans Bay
Gurnard's Head 247 Hayle FALMOUTH St Mawes
Watch 252 Ludgvan A 30 Leedstown 252 A 394 PENRYN Zone Pt
ST JUST HELIPORT Marazion FALMOUTH Mawnan FALMOUTH BAY
A 3071 PENZANCE A 394 HELSTON Rosemullion Head
esand MOUNT'S Trewavas HELFORD R Nare Pt
A 30 Newlyn BAY St Clement's Head Mawgan
Mousehole St Buryan Isle Porthleven Manacle Pt
Head Treen Poldhu Pt Mullion St Keverne 113
Mullion I A 3083 Coverack
Ruan Minor Black Head
LIZARD POINT Lizard
Point

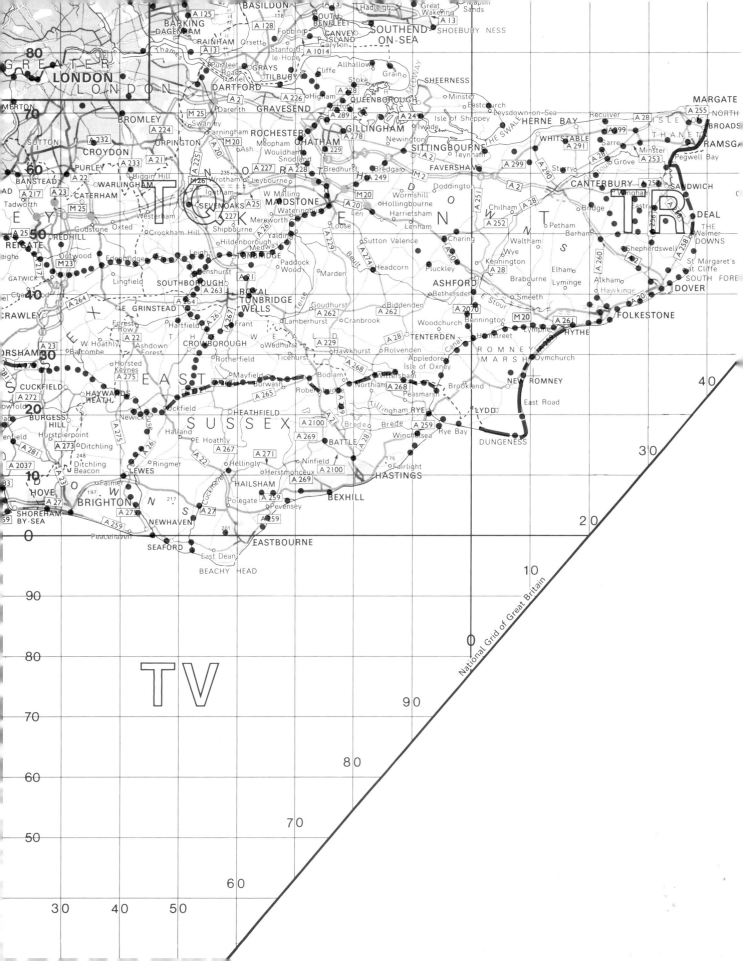

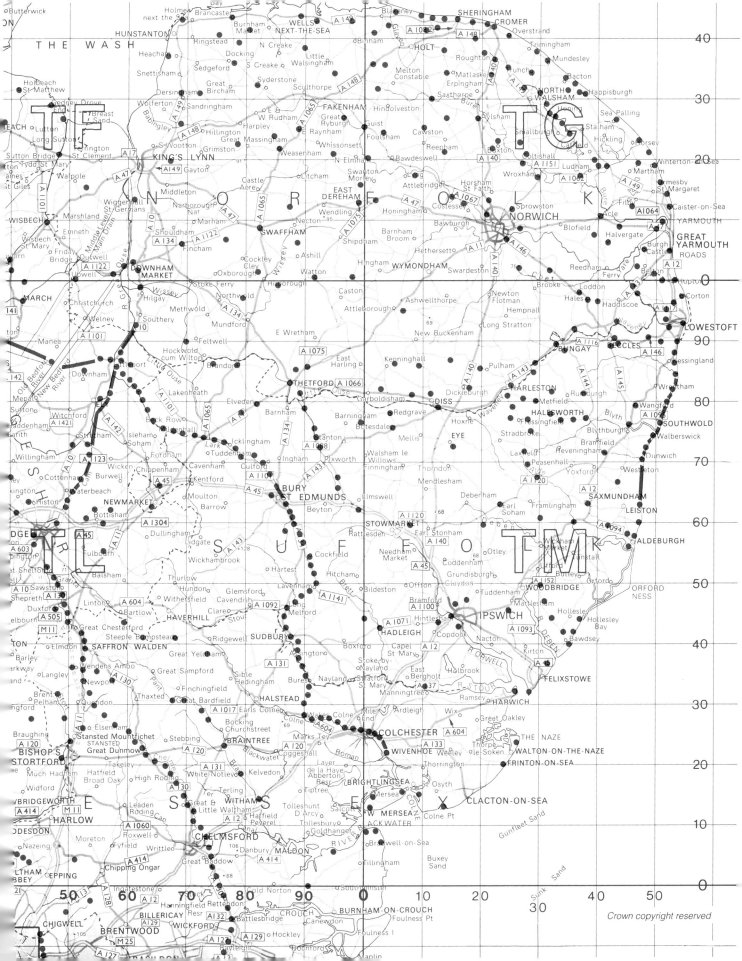

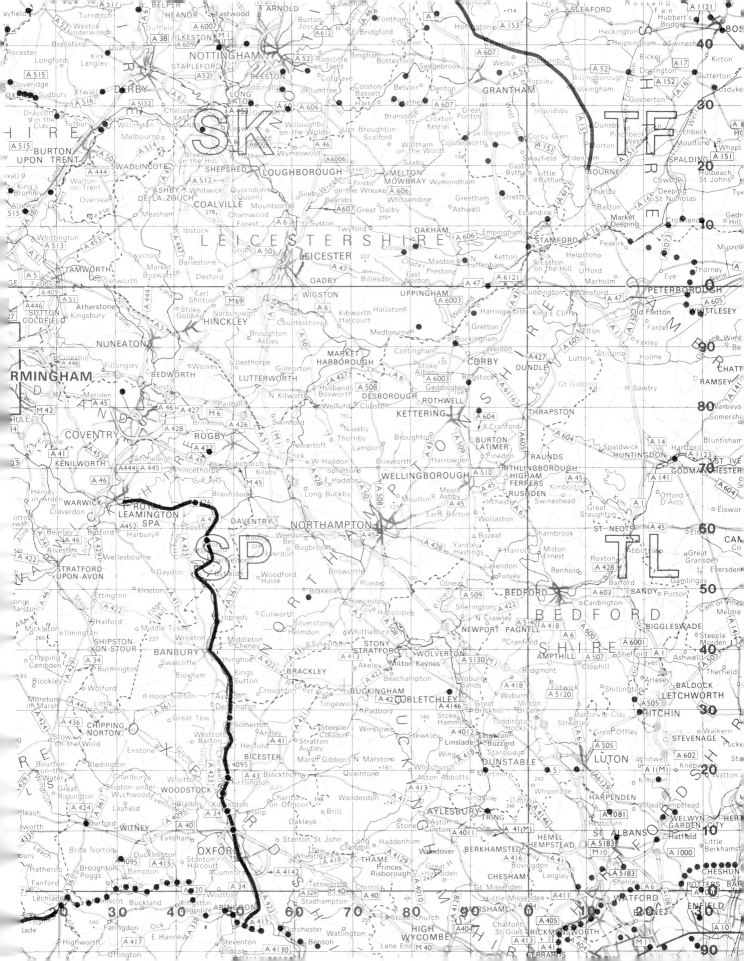

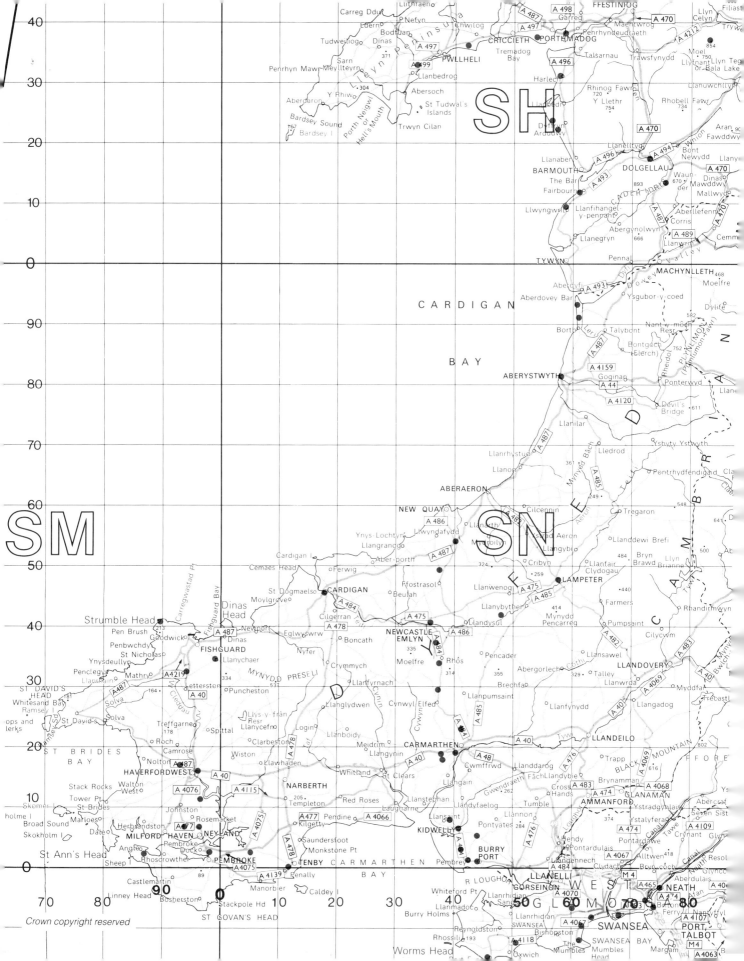

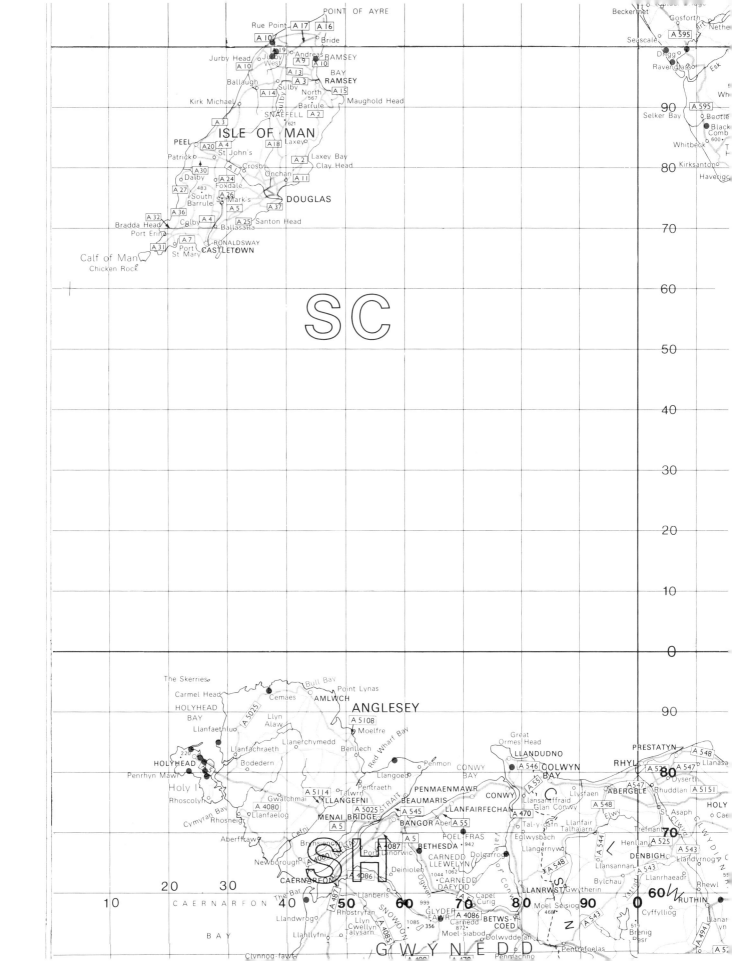

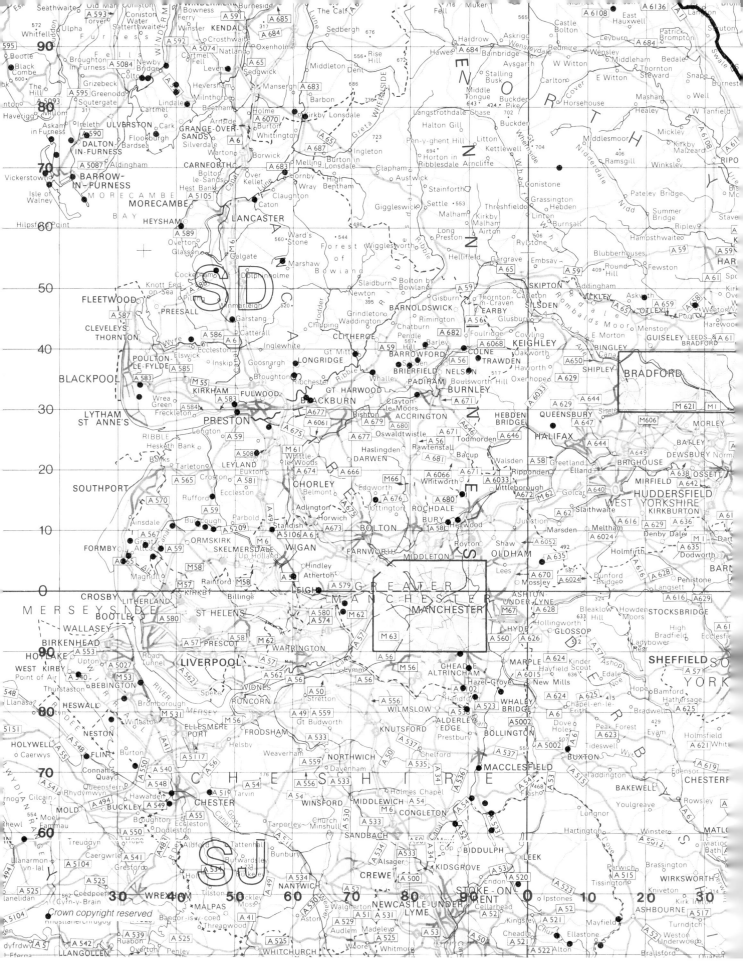

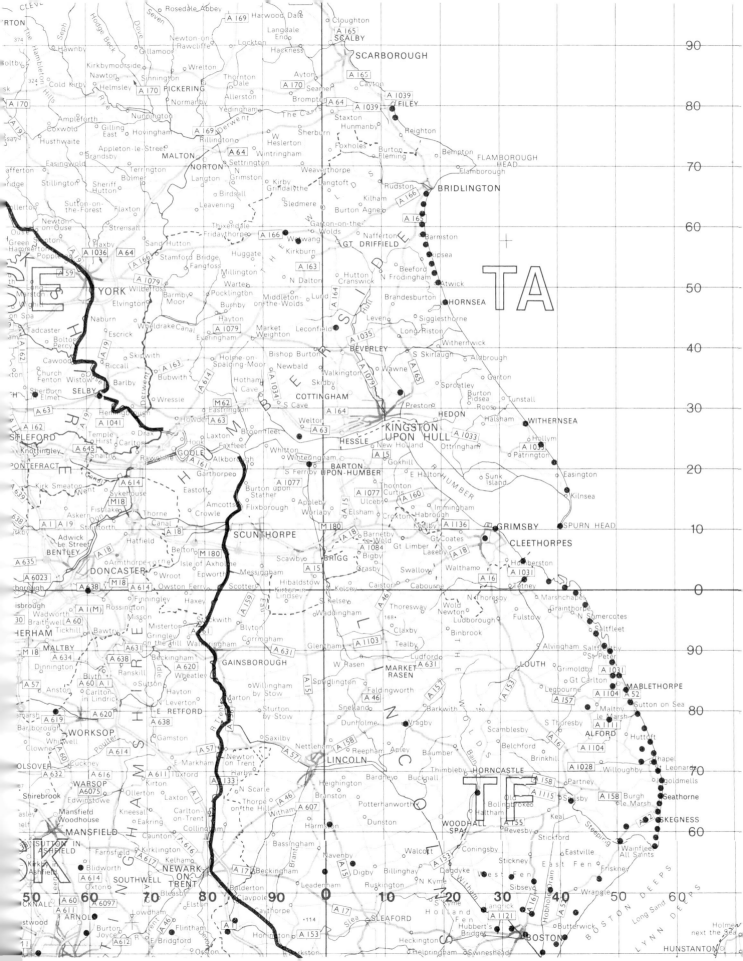

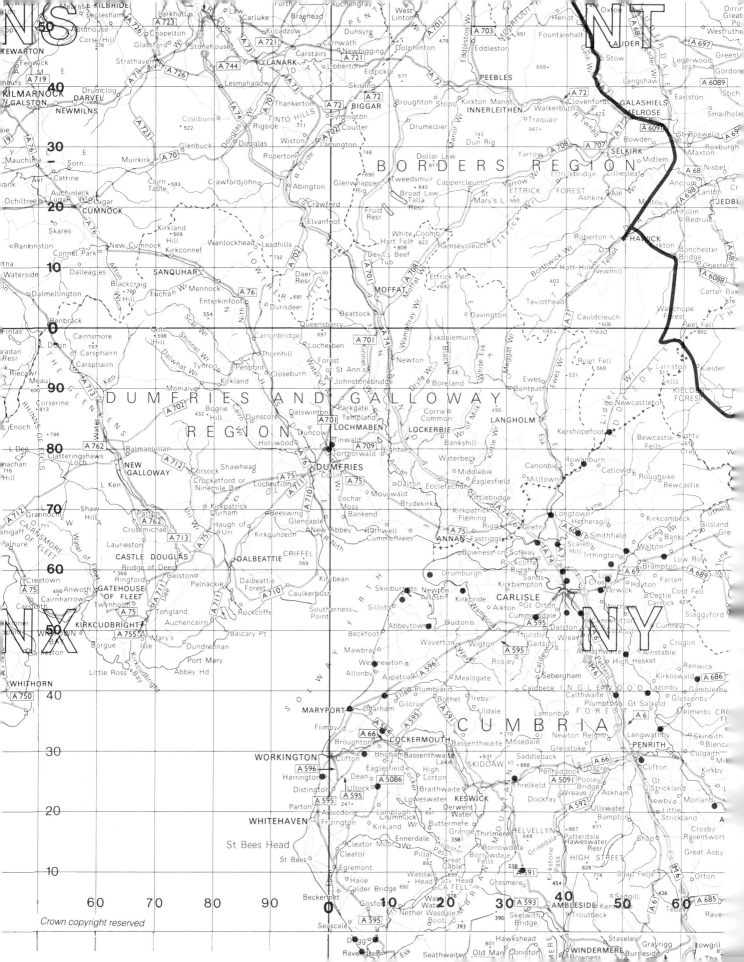

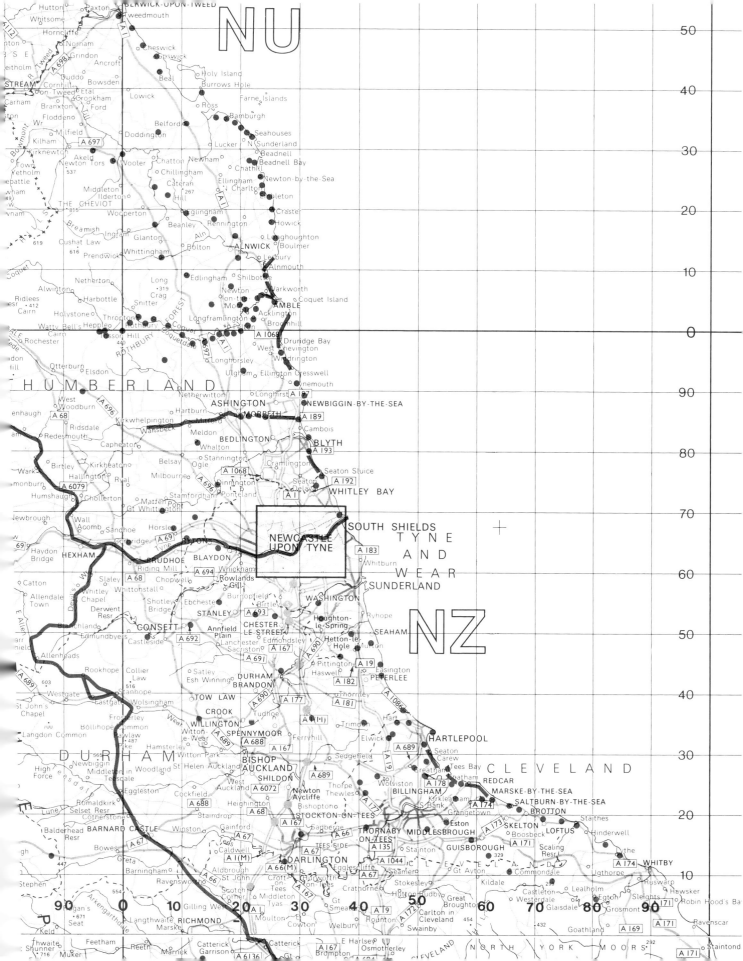

Gazetteer

THE MAP SHOWS THE positions of the 100km squares that make up the National Grid Reference system, the basis of this gazetteer. Using the six figures provided, accuracy to the order of 100 metres can be attained. However, with over 1,000 people providing information, there are bound to be errors, omissions and duplications.

The 100km squares are listed in the manner of the grid, by starting from the bottom left and working north. All Ordnance Survey maps are clearly marked with the relevant 100km square and numbers along the edge refer to the individual one-kilometre squares on the common 1:50,000 scale maps. Other scales will have full details for information.

The National Grid Reference to six figures is followed by:

First Letter: This gives plan: P = Polygonal (hexagonal, octagonal etc.)
R = Rectangular
D = Designed for site
S = Square
C = Circular
L = 'L' shaped (Section Post)
A/W = Alan-Williams steel turret
P/H = Pickett-Hamilton Fort
Martello = WW2 defences added

Second Letter: Material used in construction
C = Concrete
M = Mixture (brick/stone/breeze with concrete)

Third/Fourth Letter: Direction faced to eight points of the compass.

All-round capability signified '36' to represent 360 degrees.

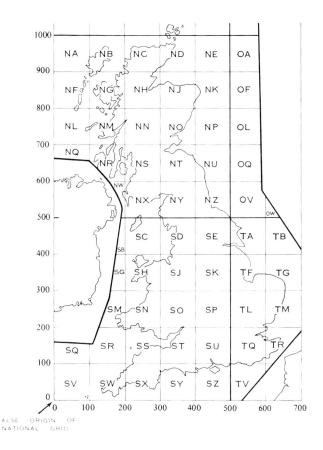

FALSE ORIGIN OF NATIONAL GRID

Other defences: The National Grid Reference followed by:

A/TB = Anti-tank Blocks
A/TC = Anti-tank Cylinders
A/TD = Anti-tank Ditch
A/TP = Anti-tank "Pimples"/Dragons Teeth
A/TR = Anti-tank Rails/girders to be inserted in road sockets
A/TW = Anti-tank Wall
A/TS = Anti-tank Scaffold
A/AP = Anti-airborne Poles (aircraft obstructions)
A/F = Airfield Defence

L/H = Loopholes in walls or buildings
AUX = Auxiliary Unit 'Hideout'
DEL = Defence Electric Light (coastal searchlight)
F/F = Flame Fougasse
smb = spigot mortar base
atr = anti-tank rifle emplacement
m.g. = machine gun position
OP = Observation Post
★ = now demolished

SV	SW	SX	SY	SY	SY
894104 DMW	352264 PMW ×2	020471 PMSE	072819	264954 PMNE	302989 PMN
898099 DMS	357263	085620	078819 SCS	265956 PMW	303984 PMNW
901099 DMSE	387220 SMSE	112643 PCN	210880 SCS	268958 PMW	303992 PMW
901105 DMSE	497412 PCN★	123515 MSE	231891 DMSE	271962 PMW	303996 PMW
912102 DMSE	510311 PMS	197016★	254900 PMSW	272943 RCSW	304998 PMW
914103 DMS	512410 PCN	199023★	254899 PMSW ×2	272944 RCNW	305992 PMN
916101 DMS	514298 PCS	202072	254902 PMSW	273964 PMW	305999 PMW
924106 DME	515298 PCS	225515 RMS	255905 PMSW	276965 PMW	308999 PMW
	548379 PMNE	257531 A/T B	256905 RCSW ×2	280966 PMW	433915
	553385 PMNW	269539 A/T B	256905 PMW	281967 PMW	448910
	557388	359538 PCS	256907 PMW	282970 PMW	491944 DMW
	557412 DCNW	425573 RCS	256909 PMW	284971 PMW	493888 PMSW
	582432 DCW	434504 PCE	257897 RMSW	286269 RCW	517884 PMS
	583403 PMW	437578 RCSW	257913 PMW	286970 PMW	521873 PMS
	583423 PMNW	440492 DMS	258915 PMSW	286971 RCW	528869 PMS
	587274 PCS	459535 RMSW	258917 PMW	289975 PMW	530866 PMSW
	582433	466535 RMS	258920 PMW	289975 RCW	528877 PMSW
	625255 PMS	469528 SCN	260922 RCW ×2	289977 PMW	537863 PMW
	640243	470527 SCS	260926 RMSW	289978 RCW	538862 PMS
	654223 RCW	487507 RCSW	260930 PMW	290977 RCW	541858 SCS
	725182 PCN	488506 RCS ×2	261925 PMSW	290979 PMW	542858 RCS
	737166 PCS	511513 PMW	261929 PMSW	290981 RCW	544856 SCS
	763263	513513 PCS	261932 PMW	291981 PMW	547853 SCS
	788278	519486 PMS	262925 PMSW	292975 PMW	550852 SCS
	789323 PME	609472 PCSE	262927 PMW	293975 PMS	552850 SCS
	793295	649439 PCE	262933 PMW	293983 PMW	555849 SMS
	797298	655442 PCSE	262935 PMW	294986 PMW	556847 SCSW
	805313	675419 PCW	262938 PMW	295975 PMSE	556848 PMS
	808217 RMS	677400 PCW	262939 PMW	296976 PMSE	563844 SCSE
	812353	714374 RMSE	262943 PMSW	297989 PMW	564842 SCSW
	819367	715375 RMS	262946 PMW	298902 PMW	568839 SCSW
	826315	732383 DMSE	262952 PMW	298979 PME	568839 A/T B
	842328	817385 PMS	263925 PMW	298980 PME	577836 SCSW
	879351	817387 DMN	263927 PME	299902 PMW	579845 A/T B
	882362	832523 PCS	263951 PMW	299982 PME	580835 SCS
	897382	894612 MSE	263954 PMW	300985 RCE	584835 SCS
	905384	936722 RMSE	264947 PMW	300992 PMN	653773 PCSW
	919744	945733 DMSE	264952 PMSE	300993 PMW	657770 PCSW
	922744	957747 --s	264953 PMNW	301983 PMSW ×2	659767 PCW
	921755	979787 SCSE		302988 PME	663763 PMSW
	921763	979789 PCNE		302988 RCE	666763 RMSW
	973413 RCS ×2				

SY	SZ	SZ	SZ	TV	SS
674808 RME	008901 SCS	198928 PCS★	624861 smb	467999 DCS★	437999 DMS
675774	010923 PMN	199929 RCS	625861 A/W	474994 DMS	601921 PME
678701 PMW	011919 PMN	201931 Dannert Wire	629993	493982 CCS	680921 DMS
679795 A/TB ×15	148930 PCN	203930 PCS★	636856	512996 CCS★	727952 A/TB ×26
681782 PCNW	018997 PCN★	205931 RCS	637894 DMSE	514477 SMW	735941 PMS
686786 PMS	018997 A/TB★	209931 PCS	680990 A/TB	514992 CCS★	752977 PMN
686786 A/TC	018998 SMW★	212947 RCNE	685995 SME	515977 RMNE	754978 PMN
679716 PMW	025833 RMSW	222931 PCS★	691997 PCSW	515978 SME	830815
679717 PMW	025834 RMW	248927 PCS★	693994 PCS	521977 RCSW	865481 DMN
671714 DM	026833 RMSW	262946 PMS	693997 PCNW	521977 RMSW	885480
692776 SCNE	026907 A/TB	263924 A/TB	696996 OP	521978 RMSW	891484
675772 SCN	033783 RCS	263968 RCS	699990 PCS ×2	521978 CCNE	911483 DCSW
695775 SCNE	033785 RCS	264924	699990 A/TB	522992 CCSW	984464 DMN
696735 RCE	034837 Sea Flame	288914 PCS	723986 RCS	525977 CCS★	984464 DMS
696739 RCE ×2	036787 A/TB ×4	290914 PCS	734985 A/TB	696062	984464 CMN
698816 A/TR ×54	036830 PCSE	295912 PMSE★	734995 PCE	770076 A/TB	990701 PMNW
698816 A/TB ×95	037828 RCNE	294933 DMS	739992 PCNE	827093 A/TB	995678
700744 SCS	037865 CCE	295940 RMS	749981 DMSW		996455 PMN
700768 SCNE	038787 CCNE	297946 A/AP	750981 DCE		996455 CMN
704745 SCS	038828 RCNE	297948 T	751982 PC		996694 PCW
704765 A/AP ×30	038829 CCE	298939 RMS ×2	751983 SCNE		997454 CMN
707756 SCE	038871 DCSE	303941 RMS	751984 A/TB		
707762 SCNE	040785 RC	305943 RMS	751989 DMS		
720905 PM36	040826 CCN	306902 PCS	775982 OP		
723901 PMNW	040826 CCE	307942 DMSE	832944 RMEW		
738896 RMS	045876 DCSE	316965 LMSW	832946 RMEW		
742816 DMS	053823 RCE	318898 DMS	833950 A/TB		
742816 PMS	059893 DCSE	324878 DMS	833952 RMW		
745819 PM	061921 DMSE	344869 PCS	835939 A/TB ×9		
770884 SMS	066897 DMSE	346856 DMS	835941 DMS		
772807 SMS	084926 LMS	346863 PCE	842934 A/TB ×40		
806803 PCS	089907 DCS	348872 PCSE	860973 DMSE		
806895 CMSW	089925 PCW	349861 PC	861968 A/W★		
818799 DMS	105922 SCS	412823 RCW	863927 ×2		
821798 DMS	107923 SMSE	483899 PCW	872960 A/TB ×6		
825797 CCE	118924 PCS	502958	873945 RMSE		
828797 SCSW	129924 SCN	507880 RCNW	873948 A/TB ×42		
854403 A/TB ×22	146932 PCS	522865	882950 RMW		
855805 CCS	147912 PCS	548775 PMSE	882950 RMSW		
870799 CCS ×2	150923 LCSE	565785 RMN	883060 SM		
871796 A/TB	153939 PMN	565785 PMNE	940989 PCS★		
871798 CCS	156934 A/TB ×48	566785 PMSW	944991 PCS		
876803 CCS	156935 PCE	585996 RMW	949993 RME		
900790 CCS	163924 PCSE	585996 A/TC ×8	951920 SCNW		
908792 CCSW	174906 RMS	587995 RMSE			
909787 CCNW	176930 P/H	591998 -CS			
911788 A/TP	177930 PCSE	592036 CMSW			
913783 RBSW	178931 SCSE	596018 SCSW			
924627 SCS	180927 SCNW	599024 RCW			
946906 SCSW	182927 PCNE	603032 SCE			
952907 SCSE	185919 A/TB	605023 SCE ×2			
988918 A/TB	185930 P/H	608864 RCN			
989919 A/TB	186919 PCSE★	608999 SCN			
	187919 RCSE	609849 RCSE			
	187921 A/TB ×2	612862 RCW			
	187921 RCSE	612887 RCSW			
	194946 DMW	613853★			

75

ST	ST	ST	ST	ST	ST
004445 CNNE	309223 PCSW	312411 RCS	319009 PMNW	327022 RCN	339046 RCNE
005431 PCN	309224 RMSW	312587 CMNW	319214 PMSW	327025 PMW	339048 PMW
005444 PCN	309279 PMS	313002 RCNW	319319 RCNW	328026 PMW	339055 PMSE
005446 DMNE	309282 RCNW	313219 PCSW	319342 PMW	328053 PCE★	339056 PME
006439	309283 RCNE	313220 PMW	320333 PMW	328204 RCSW	339057 RCW
008436	309285 PMNE	313221 PMW	321337 PMW	328463	339081 RCW
009437	309299 PMW	313350 PCW	322011 PMNW	329087 PMSW	339120 PMW
015688 PMNE	309300 RCNW	314216 RCW	322210 PMW	329201 PMW	339123 RCW
020660 ×3	309300 RCSW	314220 RCS	322325 PMW	330025 RMW	340057 PMNE
056831 PMNE	309315 PMN	314221 RCW	322328 PMW	330095 PMW	340061 PMW
008441 PM	309368	290242 PMSW	322776 DME	331026 PMW	340079 PMW
009441 PCN+	309357 PMS	290429 RCSE	323014 PMW	331028 PMW	340081 PMW
009442 PCN	309362 PME	290431 PMNE	323020 PMW	331087 RCSW	340103 PMW
081977	309371 PME	291265 PMNW	323209 PMSW	331090 PMW	340113 RCW
094957 PMW	309374 PME	291434 PMN	323210 RCSW	331091 PMW	340123 PCSW
014435	272250 PCNE	293267 PMNW	302378 PNMW	331093 PMW	340459
022434 DMN	273246 PMSW	293435 PMNW	302382 PMNW	331094 PMW	340604 PCSE
148770 DMW	274255 PMW	293435 PMNE	303229 RCNW	331095 PMW	341064 PMW
152679 PMS	275245 PMSW	293523 SMW	303277 RCNW	331196 PMW	341071 PMW
158676 PMS	275255 PMNE	293524 SMW	303277 RCS	331400 PMSW	341073 PMW
162675 PMS	276256 PMN	295523 PMW	303277 PMS	331464	341112 PMW
171454 -MN	277253 PME	296236 PMSW	303389 PMSW	331657 PCW	341124 PMNW
173675 RCS	278252 PMSE	292271 PMNW	303396 PMW	332086 PMW	341605 PCNW
173677 RCS	280243 PMSW	297234 RCSW	304229 RCSW	332094 PMN	342109 RCNW
180760 DMW	282243 PMS	197234 PMW	304280 PME	332648 PCW	342109 RCSW
180760 A/TB	282258 PMNW	298235 RCNW	304308 PMW	332653 PCW	342131 PMW
201258 RM	283259 SCN	298233 PMSW	304309 RCNW	333030 PMW	342173 PMNW
216230*	283430 PMW	298420 PMSW	304309 RCSW	334092 PMNE	342605 SCSW
250258 PMN	284434 PMNW	299232 RCS	304361 PMW	334096 PMW	343048 PMNW
270256 DM★	285259 PMNW	299232 RCW	304364 PMW	334194 PMW	343070 PMS
271252 PCSW	285429 PMW	300375 PMW	304392 PMW	334462	343138 RCSW
271253 PMW	286242 PMS	300377 PMNW	305227 RCSW	335025 PMW	343138 RCNW
271254 PMW	287426 PMS	301371 PMW	305228 PMSW	335034 PMW	343139 RCW
271256 PMNW	287431 RCNW	301372 PMW	305289 PMNW	335085 RCSW	343140 PMW
272249 PMSW	287431 RCSW	301373 PMNW	305281 RCW	335090 PMNE	343141 A/T
272250 PCSW	288262 PMNW	301373 PMSW	305304 PMW	336084 PMSW	343172 PMW
307281 RCNW	289429 RCSW	301408 PMSW	305312 PMNW	336090 PMN	343456
307284 PMNW	289431 RCNW	301414 PMW	305356 PMW	336184 PMW	344020 PME
307291 PMW	289431 RCNE	302231 PMSW	305358 PMW	337039 PMW	344137 PMSW
307369 PME	289433 PMNW	302368 PMSW	305374 PM36	337041 PMW	345071 PME
307385 PMN	309383 PMNE	302374 PMN	305408 PMS	337042 PMW	345073 PMNE
307389 PMSW	309408 PMSW	314222 PME	306282 PMNW	337053 PMSW	345144 PMNW
307397 PMNW	310228 PMNE	314350 PMSW	306313 PNMW	337055 RCW	346145 PMNW
307475 PMS	310280 PME	315005 PMW	306359 PMSW	337084 RCSW	346152 PMNW
308229 PMN	310281 PME	315216 PMSW	307226 PCSW	337084 RCW	346171 PMW
308285 PMW	310352 PMSW	315415 PMSW	307280 RCSW	337086 PME	346172 PMSE
308293 PMW	310359 PME	315416 PMN	323468 PMSW	337457	346174 PMW
308296 PMW	311002 PMW	316314 PMNW	323470 PMS	337460	347129 PMNW
308354 PMSW	311227 PMNE	317008 PMW	324016 PMW	338043 PMW	347143 RCNW
308368 PME	311278 PMSE	317216 RCW	324023 PMW	338044 PMNW	347143 RCNE
308376 PMNE	311279 PMSE	317319 PMNW	325019 PMW	338056 PMW	347166 PMW
308378 PME	311357 PMSE	317410 RCW	326205 RCNW	338058 PMW	347595 PCNW
308380 PME	312001 RCW	317410 RCS	326207 PMSW	338083 PMSW	347597 PCSW
308384 PMNE	312225 PMNE	318230 PMW	327014 RCW	338087 PME	348131 RCNW
308402 PMW	312283 PMNE	318316 PMW	327015 RCNW	338089 PMNE	348149 RCW
309001 PMW	312351 PMSW	318345 PMW	327020 PMW	338602	348150 PMW
	312411 RCW	318367 RCE	327021 RCNW	339046 RCW	348151 PCE

ST	ST	ST	ST	ST	SU
348171 RCW	439426 PMSW	563454 PMSW	721562 A/AP	945617 PMS	002384 PMS
348596 PCSE	444426 PMS	566454 PMSW	729565 A/AP	950617 PMS	002618 PC
345152 PMW	448425 PMS	576453 PMSW	729565 PMS	950617 PMS	013840 A/TC ×8
349161 PMW	449101 PME	576453 A/TB ×15	733568 PMS	950794 PME	015621 A/TB ×2
350155 PMW	464775 L/H	581451 PMS	735568 A/TB	951622 PMS	017622 PMS
351401 PMW	471419 PMS	585454 PMSW	739676 SMNW	954404 PMS	033627 PCS
351456	483422 PMS	588456 PMS	745582 PMS	955846 PMNE	039629 PMS
351609 PCSW	486422 PMS	589461 PMS	750583 PMS	957006 CCS	039629 A/TB ×4
352608 SMSE	491429 PME	591463 PMSE	753583 SMS	957786 PME	043638 PCS
353085 PMSW	492428 PMSE	596466 PMSE	755586 PMS	965617 A/TB ×4	045639 PCS
353087 PMNW	859695 PMS	596466 A/TB	757592 PMS	973825 PCNE	049979 RMNW
353149 PMSW	861611 SMSE	596796 SM–	764597 PMS	976614 A/TB ×2	054634 RMSW
353602 RMSE	863611 SMSE	598794 SMSW	766593 PCSW	976821 PCSE	057633 PMS
354147 PMSW	867409 PMS	599795 SM-	773596	978840 PCS	058625 RMSE
355145 PMSW	867613 SMSE	602814 PM-	774595 PMNE		065626 RMSE
355455 PMS	875617 PMSW	603793 SM-	783596 PMSE		067697 DMN
355597 PMS	876618 PMS	604468 PMS	783597 PMSE		069369 PMSW
355604 PMW	877618 SMS	605469 PMS	786595 PMN		073625 A/TB ×5
355605 PMNW	879417 PMS	611479 PMS	786598 PMSE		078624 PMSW
358154 RCNW	879613 A/TB	902437 PMS	788598 PMSW		083464 PCSW
358154 RCSW	881614 SME	903704 PMS	793595 SMN		083858 RCSE
359139 PMW	881617 PMS	906608 A/TC ×2	793599 PMN		084859 PCSE
360144 PMSW	882065 SMSW	909429 PMS	794601 PME		085623 PM36
360155 PCN	882622 PMSW	909932	795335 PMSW		086864 RCS
360452 PMS	883617 PMS	911665 SME	798676 RMS		089621 RMS
361137 PMS	883623 PMS	913932	800599 PMS		092620 RMSW
361152 PMNE	884616 PMS	914428 PMS	800674 CCSW		092865 RCSE
363137 PMS	885615 PMS	915672 PMS	804579 RMS		097615 PMS
365148 RCE	886623 PMSE	916925	804600 SMS		097616 RMN
366149 PME	887425 PMS	917609 PCS	804600 SMNE		098615 RMNE
367139 PME	887977 PCN	918610 PCS	804733 PCN		101616 PMS
368146 PMW	887977 A/TC ×4	918731 PMSE	806604 SMSE		101625 RCSE
371451 PMS	888623 PBSE	919611 SMSE	809603 PMS		101625 RCE
372177 PMW	889966 PCNE	919688 SMNE	811577 PMW		102314 A/TP
373451 PMS	890628 PMSE	919677 PMSE	814419 PMSE		102616 RCS
373593 SMN	891631 PMSE	920688 PMNE	815604 SMSE		108614 PMS
374450 PMS	894636 PMSE	921681	823605*		104616 A/TB
375152 PMN	895702 m.g.	922615 PCS	826598 PMSW		109878 A/TC
375593 SMN	897609 A/TC	923697 PMNE	827597 PCSW		111897 A/TC
376151 PMS	898603	924613 PCS	829607 RCS		111902 PMSE
376450 PMS	898604 PCS	925732 PMSE	829689 PCS		113607 PMS
377135 PMSW	898966 PCN	927615 PMS	830689 PC36		117928 PC36
377146 DME	899705 PMSW	931612 PM-	834416		118308 PMS
377152 PC-	900660 PME	931614 RCS	836598 RMS		118926 A/TC
377450 PMS	901615 A/TC	932614 A/TC ×2	840603 PMS		121941 RCSE
379448 PMS	901664 PME	932614 PMS	844599 PCS		128046
380447 PMS	901666 PMN	934739 PMSE	845598 PCS		128303 RMSW*
382446 PMS	901707 PMN	612488 PMS	846599 PMS		129047
402447 PMSW	505434 PMS	612806 PMW	849609 PMSW		129304 L/H*
406445 PMSW	541239 PCSW	613805 PME	849694 PMNE*		135141 SCSE
441443 PMSW	542239 PCN	621507 PCSE	851600 SMS		138302 DMNW*
415440 PMSW	542964	622500 PNSE	851601 PMN		138373 PCW
419438 PMSW	543240 PCSE	629511 SMS ×2	851601 PMS		141147 PCN
422435 PMSW	548149 PCS	707556 PMS	856612 PMS		141371 PCSW
427432 PMSW	561455 PMSW	708555 PMS	942859 A/TB		142148 PCNW
431431	561455 A/TB	716559 PMS	943867 PMNE		142614 PMS
435428 PMSW	549903 PMS	718560 PMS	944862 PMSW		143141 PCW

SU	SU	SU	SU	SU	SU
143144 LCW	235633	308392 PMSE★	440666 PCSW	516034 SMSW	617015 SCSE
143145 LCW	237633 PCS	309385 PM36	440666 PCSE	517131 DM36 ×4	619686 RME
144137 LCSW	238630 A/TD	311681 PMS	441161 smb	525662 PCS	621781 PCSW
144137 PCNW	239982 PCW ·	315681 PMS	443666 PCS	526130 PM36	623778 PCSW
145137 LCSW	245625 A/TB	323683 A/TB	447160 PCNW	527943 RMSE	624689 RME
145146 RCN	247622 A/TB	351682 RMW	447667 PCS★	529663 PCS	625772 PCSW
145148 SCN	249257 PMSW	351682 RMSE	448170 PMW	530664 RCS	626693 RME
147054 SMNE	249986 PCSW	352683 PMS	449161 SMSW	538663 RMW	627003 PCSW
147153 PCN	253258 PM-	355997 PCSE	452669 PCS	541939 PCSE	630769 PCSW
147312 RMN	253989 PCS	357682 PMS	452966 RMS	542020 SCS	635765 SMS
148127 SCSW	256270 PMN★	362215 A/TB	454975 RC-	542941 RCW	637699 RMSE
148372 PCN	258269 PM-	362680 A/TB	454349 PC36	548948 RMW	637699 RMNW
148616 PMS	258622 CMSE	369002 PCSW	455669 PCS	548948 A/TB ×7	638748 RCSW
149129 PCN	258984 PCS	370137 RMNS	457173 PCNE	550663 RCW★	638749 RCNE
149309 RMNE	258987 PCS	372675 PCS	457348 PC36	550663 RCSE★	638058 SCN
150616 PMSW★	259269 PMN	377672 A/TB	458173 PMSE	551663 RCE	638525 ★
151142 DCS★	261622 RME	377373 PCS	458357 PC36	552663 PCSE	638526 L/H
151328 PCS	263269 PM-	383671 A/TB	459174 LME	563664 ★	638744 RCNE
151367 PCN	264624 A/TB	387023 DMW	459673 PCS	570938 RMW	639065 smb
152153 PCN★	265268 PM-	388022 RMSE	460193 DMN	571665 RCE	639744 A/TC ×4
153133 L/H	266269 PM-	388023 DME	460193 smb	571666 RCW	639744 RCE
153547 PCNW	266627 PMS	388672 PCS	461673 PCS	572047 PMS	639749 RCNW
153613 PMS	267268 PM-	390672 RCS	462342 PCS	572050 SCS	639748 RCSE
157340 PCN	268269 PM-	392672 PCS	463098 PCNW	572050 PMN	639757
155612 PMS	269988 PCS	395144 A/TP	464343 PC36 ×2	577666 RMW	639764
157153 PCE	270267 PM-	397672 RCSE	464360 PC36	578936 RMSE	639767
157612 PCS	270630 A/TC ×9	298385 P/H★	465672 PCS	579934 RMSE	640749 RCN
158611 PMSE	271268	398672 PCS	467073 DC36	580665 PCW	641742 A/TC ×4
158297 A/TD	272268	401148	467348	584666 RMW	640751 RCNE
159607 A/TC ×10	272632 A/TC ×10	406026 A/TC ×6	468069 DC36	587068 CCS	640762
162174 RMN	274636 PMSE	406673 PCSE	470671 PCSW★	588065 CCSW	642742
162174 DMS	277267	411673 RCSW	471157 SCNE	589933 RMSW	644740 RCW
162175 SMN	277992 PCSW	412995 RCS	471343 PC36	590514 RMS	643741 RCNW
162493 PM36	278642 PMW	412996 RCN	471348 RC36	590666 RCNE	645740 RCNW
163611 PMS	278989 m.g.	414157 PMN	471361 PC36	590667 RCSW	646733 PCSW
163613 PMSW	281267 A/TC ×10	415990 RCSE	471659 PMS	591022 RCNW	647705 RMSE
170619 RMS	281267 A/TR ×15	419671 PCS	472154 PMSE	592068 CCS	647731 PCW
175399 PCSW	283263 PME	420161 PCN	473346 PC36	594019 SCSW	648726 RCW
183410 PCN	283993 m.g.	421988 RCNW	474361 PC36	594023 RCN	648728 RCW
187687 PCSE	284996 RCS	421989 RCSW	475673 PCS	594046 RCE	648735 RCW
189693 DCNW	286262 PME	422159 pc-	478068 PMNW	594922 PCNW	649721 RCSW
190403 PCS	286994 RCS	424671 PCSW	478347	595020 RCNE	651721 RCSW
190625 RMS	287995 m.g.	424671 PCSE	478357 PCN	595838 RCW	653714 RCW
194627 RMS	288265	425165	479356 DCSW	597847 DM-	653044 DEL
195404 PCN	297391 PCSE	425980 RCSE	480012 L/H	598671 RCW	654716 RCSW
201689 PMNE	299081 A/TB	425981 RCNW	482675 PCS	599672 PCS	656708 RMW ×2
201689 PMSW	299388 P/H	426116 RMSE	482965 RCNW	602672 PC-	659044 CMNE
218636 PMS	299393 DM36	428116 RME	484058 RCS	602925 RMSE	659570 SMW
218993 PCSW	299395 DM36	430152 PCNW	484965 RCS	605921 RM-	662710 PCSW
222634 A/TB	299671 A/TB	432667 SCS	488051 SCW	606672 PCS	664043 RCN
222992 PMS	300375 m.g.	432668 PCS	495139 CCSE	608673 PCS	665034 P/H
228633 PMS	300398 PMSW	432977 RCNW	499665 SCW	609039 RMS	667042 m.g.
228633 A/TB ×24	301389 P/H★	432977 RCSW	502665 PCS	609674 RCS★	668043 PCSW
231982 PMS	301392 RCSW	435666 PCS	502951 PCSW	610681 RCS	668564 SMS
234272 A/TD	302402 PMNW	438975 RCNW	505663 PCSW	611002 SCS	667709 RMNW
234634 PMS	302675 PMSE	439154 PMS	507947 RCE	614684 RMW	669585 SME
234981 PCW	306375 PMSE	439158 PM-	515034 SMSW	615794 PCSW	670755 RCSW

SU	SU	SU	SU	SU	SU
672033 P/H	741551 PMW	784548 PMS	834472 RMS	869444 SMSW	909588 PCW
673039 P/H	742553	785547 PMNE	834473 PMSW	870455 A/TB ×12	909588 A/TB ×12
674708 RME	742583 PMSW	785547 PMS	833474 PMSW	870512 CMSE	911455 A/TC ×8
676708 PMSW	742584 PMSW	785548 PM-	834476 PMN	871455 DMS	914552 PME*
680043 DMSW	742590 PMS	787546 PMNW	833477 PMNW	871456 PMS	915561 A/TC
680707 RMS	742616	788515 PMSE	834485 PMSW	871456 RMNW	918674 PME
681708 RMNE	743553 PMW	709517 A/TB ×26	835468 PMNW	873446 CCSW	921461 A/TC ×4
683581 PMW	743560 PMW	790524 PMS	835473 PMS	874435 PBW	921561 RCNW
691685 DMS	743577 PMSW	791514 PMS	835483 PMS	874434 A/TB ×2	921562 PCSE
692044 DMSE	743587 PMSW	791523 PM-	835484 PMSW	875433 RMSE	921563 PCSE
693702 RM-	744491 PMS	792503 PCSW	835507 A/TC	875433 PMW	921563 A/TB ×2
696542 PMS	744552 PMNE	793486 PMW	836473 PMSE	875434 PMW	922695 PMSE
703654 PMS	744555 PMSW	794505 PMS	836476 PMSW	875461 Aux	923439 PMS
703666 PMW	744559 PMW	796501 PMSW	836478 PMW	875510 CM36	923440 PMS
703674 PMSW	744581 PMSW	796549 PMSW	836481 PMW	875512 A/TB	926443 PMS
704659 PMNW	744581 PMS	797499 RMN	836482 PMSW	875514 CMSE*	932562 PCSE
704670 PMW	745554 PMW	797515 SMS	837471 PMS	875514 CMSW*	933578 RMNE
705652 PMS	746647	798500 PMS	838466 PMW	878450 CCN	936008 PCSE
705657 PBMS	747550 PMS	801503 PM-	842014 RCSW	878477 PMSE*	936577 RCSW
706602 PMW*	747579 PMS	804506 PM-	843528 SMS ×2	878513 CCSW*	936578 RCS
707628 RMNW	747580 PMW	805555 PMSW	844466	878513 CME*	937436 PMW
707655 PME	748030 SCW	806506 PM-	845467 PMSW	879447 RCS	938006 PCSE
708659 RMSW	748544 PM-	806556 PMW	846485 PMSW	879559 PME	938437 RMS
708677 PMSW	749544 PM-	808508	847415 PCS*	881465	938567 RCSE
711384 A/TB ×3	749547 PM-	808513	847469 RMNE	881517 A/TB ×4	938576 RCSE
711538 PMS	750027 RMSW	809505	848420 A/TB	883519 A/TB ×2	938578 RCS
712680 PMNW	751074 SC-	809507	848468 PMSE	887491 DMS	939436 PMS
713015 RM-	753022 PMS	811492 PMSW	848469 A/TB ×10	887538 A/TB	941572 PCS*
714012 PCSW	753548 PMSW	813494 PM-	849526 A/TC	888627 PMSE	942436 PMS
714417	755038 SMNW	813504 RM-	851478 PMNE	889565 mined	944579 RCSE
714686 RMSW	763527 RMS	814495 PM-	851552 PMW	892564 RCSE	945571 RC-
715025 PCW	765012 PMSW	814503 PM-	851461 PMSE	893482 A/TD	945776 CCNW
715651 PMS	766011 SMSE	815494 PCS	851469 PMNE	893535 PMN	947436 SMW
717017 PM-	766531 PMS	815504 RM-	851853 PCN	893537 PME	958572 PCN
718045 *	767012 PME	816493 PMSW	852474 PMS	893583 DMNW	959446 PMS
720017 PM-	767033 PMNE	816501 PM-	852527 RMS ×2	893539 PME	959446 A/TB ×2
720038 RMN	767037 SCE	816502 PM-	853549 RMSW	894528 PME	963445 DMS
720653 PM-	767525 PMS	816668 DME	854600 SCSW	894534 PMS	968573 RMS
724016 PM-	767527 PMSE	817504	855558 PM-	895328 smb	969572 RM-
728510 PCNW	769531	822492 PMSW	855600 PMSW	896398 A/TC	970444 PMSE
729511 DCNW	776522 A/TB ×200	822495 PMS	855793	899440 PMS	973585 PCW
730508 PMW	777518 A/TC ×3	822497 PM-	858476	899447 RMS	976015 DM-
732089 LMSE	777520 A/TB	823503 RM-	859074 A/TBX ×100	901063 CM36	976581 A/TC ×4
732089 RMS	777520 A/TC ×6	824503 PMS ×3	859473 RMS	901440 PMS	977444 PMSE
733091 RMS	777524 A/TC ×66	827554 PM-	859603 RCW	901440 RCS	977583 PCNE
733092 LMNE	777669 RMN	828459 A/TC	861466 A/TC	903442 PMSW	978529 A/TC ×4
733092 RMSE	778517 A/TC ×8	828459 PMS	861479 PMW	904437 DCS	979578 A/TC ×6
733576 A/TC ×4	778520 A/TB ×45	828488 PMSW	862465 PMSE	904441 PMS	979579 DMS
734577 A/TC ×3	778524 PMW	829487 PMSW	862469 A/TB	904441 RCS	983578 A/TC ×6
736081 *	778524 A/TB ×4	832485 PMSE	862466 PMSW	904442 RCS	984449 CCS
736568 PMW	778526 PCW	832555 PM-	863465 PMSW	905065 *	988453 CCSW
737999 PMS	778730 PME	833476 A/TC ×3	863558 DM-	905328 A/TC	990454 CCSE
738080 LMS	778739 PMS	833485 PMS	864463 PMS	905436 PM36	991442 CC-
739544 PMN	779514 PM-	833487 PMSW	866463 PM-	905438 A/TC	994464 CCSE
740590 PMSW	781533 A/TB ×3	833536 RMS	868448	905582 PCSE	994468 CCSE
740593 PMSW	782513 PMSW	833536 PMS	868452 SMSW	907437 RM36	995472 CCE
740611 CCSW	783513 SMS	834468 RMN	868460 RMW	908438 L/HX8	999479 A/TB ×3
	784513 SMS	834472 PMW	869443 RM-	909339 smb	

| --- | --- | --- | --- | --- | --- |
000478 CCSW	054808 PCSW	118953 PCN	198509 PMS	239476 PMSW	286452 PMS
000480 CCSW	056937 PCW	118955 DMN	199176	239479 PM-	287455 PMS
002478 CCS	057593	118955 DCN*	201051 m.g. ×4	240476 PMS	288450 PMS
003042	058488 PMS	118969 PMNW	201447 RMS	240478 PMS	288453 PMW
003472 CCSW	060390 A/TB	118974 PMNW	201447 SMS	240884 PM-	289918 PCN*
003500 A/TB	061487 PMS	119491 PMS	202502 PMSE	241475 PMSE	290997 SMSE
006393 PCE	061939 PCNE	119954 DCN	203049 RMNW	241476 PM-	291450 PMS
006474 CCS	064488 PMS	120443 L/H ×3	203059 PMS	243758 PMS	292906
008473 CCW	065014 L/H	120491 PMS	204498 PMS	244474 PMSW ×2	293451 PMS
009391 PCE	065942 PMN	120980 PMN	205058 PMS	245291 PMSW	293960
011009 L/H	066932 PMN	121735	205059 PMS	245758 PCS	296433 A/TC ×60
011042 RCSW	067487 PCSW	122019 SCS	205059 PM36	246290 A/TB ×14	296446 PME
011374 CCS	067609 A/TB	122031 m.g.	205059 RCS	246910 PMNW	297450 PMN
012475 CCSW	068485 PMS	123495	206817 PC-	247472 PMSE	298486 PMS
015476 CCS	071485 PMS	123982 PMNW	207054 PMW	247478 PM-	299445 PM-
017474 CCSW	073943 PMN	125495 PMS	207496 PMSW	248471 PMS	299589 A/TB ×5
022478 CCS	072491 PCSW	125732 PMS	207497 ×2	249278 PMSW	301059 DCN
024475 DME	072485 PMS	125819 PMSW	208053 PMEW	249279 PMS	302443 PMS
025131 PCN	073015 DEL	126496 PMS	208492 PMSW	249469 PMSW	303281 PCS
025479 CCS	073941 PMN	126984 PCN*	208493 PMSW	249474 PM-	306444 PMNE
027477 CCNW	075486 PMS	128496 PMS	209495 PMS	250469 PMSW	306602 A/TB ×50
028185 CCS	075940 PCN	138120 PMS	209609 PMS	251274 A/TB ×4	307442 PME
028476 CC36	077485 PMS	140312 A/TB	210496 PMS	251475 PM-	308283 PMS
029105 RCS	079941 PCN	142025 SCS	211183 RCS	252275 PMS	308307 PMS*
029797 A/W	082327 RMS	143974 PM36	211492 SMS	252471 RMS	309438 PMSE
030184 PCW	083486 PMS	149025 RCS	211818 PMW	252473 PMS	315634 A/AP
030478 CC36	084327 RMSW	154024	212155 DCE	253472 PMS	316702 PC-
031722 A/TB ×3	084942 RMN	160953 PMNE	212497 PMSE	255476 PMS	321443 PMS
033484 PCS	086489 PMS	164995 *	212498 PMSE	255902 PC-	323443 PMS
035480 CC-	086997 DCN	168303 RMSW	212818 PMNW	256475 PMS	323579 PME
036484 PCS	087193 RCS	170522 PMSW	212830 RMS	256504 A/TB ×90	324281 RMS
037486 PCS	087258 A/TB ×4	171515 PMS	213498 PMSE	256517 F/F	326580 PMSE
040189 PCS	087488 PMS	171617 PCS	213764 PCS	258471 RCS	332577 PMW
041913 PMNW	088945 RMN	175511 RMSW	213818 PCS	259471 RMSW	333132
042186 PCS	089488 PMSW	175512 PMSW	213818 PMS	259474 PMS	339275 RMS
042482 PCS	090944 PCN*	176033 RCS	214723 SMSE	259757 RMS	339444 RMSW
042484 PCS	090957 DCN	178692 DMS	215159 PCSE	260471 PMSW	340441 RMSW
042905 PMW	092484 PMS	178693 *	215159 DME	261471 PMSW	341441 PMS
044930 PMNW	092941 DMNE	181035 RCS	222906 PC-	262460 PMS	341443 PMSW
045187 PCS	098014 SMS	185036 RCS*	225487 PMNE	262471 PMSW	342686 RMNS
045805 PCS	100015 RCS*	186106 DMS	225491 PMSW	263466 PMS	343442 PMSW
045932 PCE	101771	187292 PMSW	225494 PMW	263467 PMSW	343444 PME
046486 PCS	102947 PMNW	189037 RCS	225496 PMW	263470 PMSW	346442 PMS
047904 SMSW	106758 PMSW	190176	226486 A/TB ×7	264278 RMS	346445 PMSE
048489 PCS	107329 PMS	192834 PC- ×2	226488 PMSE	264464 PMSW	347444 PMSE
049833 DMN	108118	193508 PMS	228488 PMSE	265455 PMS	348442 PMSW
049836 DMS	108488 PMS	193785 PME	229488 PMS	265471 PMS	348443 PME
049893 PCW	110487 PMS	194088 RME	230487 PMSE	266277 A/TB ×2	349446 PMS
050480 PMS	111488 PMS	195774 PCS	231488 PMSE	266278 RMS	352262 RMSW
050889 PCW	111953 DMN*	195839 PCS	231602 A/TP	272455 PMS	352262 A/TB ×2
051933 PCW	113487 PMS	196777 PCS ×2	234483 PMSW	273451 PMS	354655 A/TB
052847 PMS	114746 PMSW ×2	196793 PMS	234485 PMSW	273452 PMS	358468 PMS
052875 PCSW	113953 PCN*	196838 PCS	235480 PMSW	278475 A/TB ×7	359448 *
052878 PCNW	114726	197055 PMNW	235483 PMSW	279275 PMS	360449 *
053802	117490 PMS	197057 PCNW	236484 PMSW	282274 A/TB ×2	361450 RMSW
053871 PCW	117966 PMNW	197658 PMS*	237476 PM-	282276 RMS	361450 RMSE
054935 PMN	117969 SCN	198498 PMS		285779 RMS	362450 PME

TQ	TQ	TQ	TQ	TQ	TQ
362452 PMSE	415619	462206 SMN	517431 PMSW	534769 PCNE★	579467
364452 RMSW	415884 PM-	465209 PMS	517432 PMW	535050 PME★	581328
365453 PMS★	416090	465460	517434	536053 PC36	589251 PMSW
366452 RMSE	417447 A/TB	466557	517444	536770 ★	589353
368452 RMSW	416452 PMS	467798	517458	537056 PM-	589357
368701 PCS	418088 PMS	469209 PMS	517780 PCN★	537347	591465 PCS
369450 PMSW	419065 PMSE	470209 PMS	518364 RMNE	537754 PCN★	591471
369450 PMSE	419087 PMNE	472455 ★	518421	538439	593470
370453 PMS	420448 ★	475453 PMSE	518441	540298 RME	594471
370456 PMSE	420455 PMN	477453 PMS	518448	540345	601468 PCS
372450 RMSE	421065 PMSE	478210 PMSE	518453	540781 PCN★	602254 PMS
372451 RM★	421128 PMS	480454	519363 PCN	541301	603401 RCS
373990 PMW	422051 PMSE	482234 PME	520268 PCW	541302	607361 PMNW
374450 RMSW	422131 PMS	482236 PME	520364	540337	607472 PCS
375450 PMSE	422449	488455	520412	542051 PMS	608456 PME
375991 PMNE	422455 PMN	489456	520431 PMS	542303	610440
377451 PMSE	423082 PMNE	489356 PCSE	520436	542437	613413
378452 RMSE	424050 PMSE	491358 PCSE	521414 PMS	542442	613457 PMS
380452 RMSW	424078 PMS	492356 PCE	521467	543338	617403 PCSE
381452 PMSE	424080 PMN	492458	522364	543342	617686
384245 A/TB	425079 PME	493231 SME	522431 PMSE	543445	619408 DCSE
383455	425229 PMW	493460 PMS	522432 PMSW	543448	622043 RCSE
384453 PME	425231 PMSW	493462 PMS	522467 PCNE	543450	622472
387453 RME	425451 PMS	494077 SMS	522467 PCW	543779	625408 PMS
387453 RMS	426138 PMS	494461 PMS	523364	544305	625472 RCS
388066	427036 PMSE	496462	523260 PMS	544339	626426
389462 RMS	428144 PMS	498464	524272 PMSE	544455	626473 PCS
389454	428149 PMS	500462	524432 RMSE	545335	627069 A/TB ×13
390451 PMS	428215 RMSW	501458	525415 PMS	545462 A/TP ×5	627472
391661 A/TB	429148 PMSE	503457 PMS	525433 PMSE	546308	628260 PMS
392451 PMS	429453	503850	526416 PMSE	546309	629473 smb
392453 PMS	431457 PMS	504384	526434 PMNE	546345	629474 PMS
394453 RMSW	432139 PMS	504389	526436 PMN	546459 PCSE	635008 A/TW
394458 PMS	433148 PMS	505395	526443	547313	635013 PCS★
394907 PMN	434150 PMNW	505456 PMS	527363	547314	635474 PMS
397452 PMS	434450	506395	527415 PMS	547337	637069 CCS
398454 RMW	435148 PMS	507397	527433 A/TB	547453 PMSE ×2	638022 DCS
399452 ★	436147 PMS	508556	527467 PCW	547457 PCS	638268 PMS
400908 PMN★	438207 RME	509456 PMS	528430 PMSE	548455 PMSW	641011 A/TW
402087 PMSE	439207 A/TB	510369 RMSE	528435 PMS	549317	641473 PMSE
402451 ★	440454 ★	510400	528751	550328	641473 PMSW
403086 PMSE	443465	511369 RME	529288 SME	552324	643015 CCEW
404238 RMSE	444180 PM	511370 RMNE	529363	557462	644012 Martello
405100 DMS	447182 PMS	511456	529416	559463 RMS	644016 CCEW
405451 ★	448181 PMS	512366 RMNE	529428 PMSE	562259 PCS	646048 DMS
405759 PMW	448182 PMW	512536 RCS	529430 PMSE	562462 PMS	646473 PMS
406235 PMSW	449461 PCSE	513368 RMNE	529439	563461	647012 PC36
410449 PMS	450002 DME	513369 RMSE	530354	564461	647021 PC36M
411075 PMSE	450461	513456	531418	566460	648027 PC36
412067 PME	451207 A/TB	514367 RMNE	531425 PMSE	569458	648473 CCS
412738 PMS	451462	515365 RMNE	531426 PMSE	569461	648735
413066 PMSE	453208 SME	515367 RMNE	532352	572462	650745
413074 PMSE	454467	516406	532439	573004 DMS	651031 PC35M
413451 PMS	455464	516455	533420 PMSE	574007 RMS	652062 CCSE
413615	456461	517264 SMNE	533422 PMSE	573463	654074 SMS
413754	458454	517267 PME	533462 A/TP ×3	574111 RCW	654473
415453 PMS	460205 SMN	517365 RMNE	534349	576465	655475

TQ		TQ		TQ		TQ		TQ		TQ	
656078	SM36	708644	PME	745881	PCNE	763976	PME	797133	A/TB ×100	896847	A/TB ×2
656268	PMS	708661	PME	746014	PC36	763983	PMS	798727	CCW ×3	903944	PCE
657078	SM36	708743	PMN	746160	A/TB	765079	A/TC	805590	PCS	904942	PCE
657079	SM36	709529	SCS	747029	RCNE	765547	A/TB	807707	PC-	907474	PCS
657475	PMS	709635		747639	RCE	765709		808588	PM-	909175	
661473	PMS	710535	PMS	747645	RC-	765975	RMS	809598	PCS	909476	PCNW
661475	PMS	710758	PCN	747648	RCE	765979	PMSE	810599	PCSE	911939	PCE
662754	*	710758	A/TB ×6	749160	DMSE	766688	A/TB	811593		913159	SCSE
668479	*	711268	PCS	749549	PCS	766713		812589	PCSE	916176	PCSE
668555		711823	PMSE	749702		766741	RMSW	813500	PMNE	916181	SCSE
669470	*	712536	RCS	749738	RMNE	766741	A/TB ×6	813591	SCSE	916256	RMW
669481	*	712606	PME	749738	RMNW	766974	RMSE	813603	PMN	916873	PME
669554	PMN	713755	PCN	749738	A/TB ×6	766976	RMSE	813612		917163	OP
670480	PMS	714539	PMS	749873	SCE	767703	×2	815778	PCN	917166	PCSE
672482	PMS	715612	PME	750242	DMS	767710		816602	PMNW	917696	SCSE
677487	PCS	717865	PMW	750691		767741	RME	816596	PCNW	919199	PCSE
679487	PCSE	718541	PMS	750876	RMS	767741	A/TB ×6	817603	CCE	919466	A/TC ×2
680487	PMS	718589	PME	751549	RMS	768965	PMN	819598	PMS	922855	
680758	PCS	720757	PM-	751571	PME	769245	PMSE	819603	PMNE	924206	
681053	Martello	720864	PMS	751576	PME	769712	PMS	819608	CCSE	924208	PCSE
681758	PCS	722671	PCSE	751583	RMSE	769965	PME	819782	PCN	925455	DM-
683491	PCS	723540	PMS	751686		770700		820601	PME	928456	PCNW
684494	PCE	725540	RMS	752886	PCE	770959	PME	821610	CCSE	928840	A/TB ×18
684506		725540	PMS	752998	PME	771246	SMSE	823613	CCSE	932226	PCSE
685265	PMS	725675	PCSE	753584	RMS	771956	PMNE	823787	PCN	933840	PMS
685519	PCE	725732	PMN	753876	SMS	772712		824783	PCN	935203	SCSE
686506	PCNE	725734		753879	PMSE	773211	A/TB ×128	827787	PCN	935237	PCSE
686513	PCE	725742		754564	PME	773742		830443	A/TB ×2	936245	PCS
687495	PCNE	725864	PME	754568	PME	773956	RMSE	831784	PCN	942255	PCSE
687516	PCE	726078	PCSE	754569	A/TB ×9	773957	PME	831852	DCW	942264	SMSE
687523	PME	726539	RCSW	754738		774733	PMN	832542	RCE	945487	PCE
688497	PMSE	729583	PMS	755701	PME	775736	RMNW	832785		946267	PMS
688504	PCNE	729588	RCN	755716	PMNE	775736	A/TB ×6	833271	RMS	947486	PC*
689496	PCS ×2	729589	RCW	755736	RMNE	775739	RMNE	833788		948182	PCSE
690058	SMS	729677	PCE	755736	A/TB ×6	775950	PCE	834549	SCE	950492	PCN
690769	SCN	731750	PCE	755871	RCSE	776733	PMN	837615	CCSE	952189	PCS
691499	RCSE	732536	PCS	755995	PMSW	776699		852618	SMSE	952490	PC-
691504	PCNE	732732	PME	756565	PMSE	777204	RMSE	863636		956188	PCSW
691536		733535	PMS	756716	PMNE	777213	A/TB ×61	863897	PMSE	957188	PCSW
692502	PCE	734050	PCNW	756741		777734	PMN	864638		957292	PCSE
693499	A/TB ×4	734535	PMS	757556	A/TB	779735	PMN	864937		960301	
693501	PCE	734585	PME	757704	PCS	780712	PMS	865895	CC36	960186	RCS
693535	L/H	734743	PME	757735		782730		865897	CC36	961186	SCS
694749	PCN	734750	RMS	757868	PME	782731		867889		961479	PC*
697529		735738		757996	PMNE	783533	RC-	868277	RMS	963485	PC*
701520	PMS	736040	PCSE	758683		785254	DMS	872641	SMSE	965186	SCS
701769	L/H	736740	RMNE	758876	RMS	785707		872643	SMSE	966504	A/TC
701789	SC36	736744		758905	RC-	786792		875898	CC36	969467	PCS
703530	*	736761	PCN*	758908	RC-	787672		876895	CCN	976183	
705533	RCS	738537	PMW	759983	PMSE	788727	PMN	877889	CC36	978443	PCSE
705534	PMS	740539		759994	PMNW	788727	A/TB ×2	882897	SMSE	979315	PCSE
705657	PME	741651	RC-	760889	SCE	791722	PMNE	887259	RMW	984756	PMSW
706078	PSC*	742540		760976	PMSE	792716	PMN	887772	A/TB ×100	985322	PCS
706638	PME	742584	PME	760988	PME	792717	RCNE	890135	OP	987329	PCN
707269	PMS	743582		763686		792717	A/TB ×9	890876		990321	PCS
708623	PME	744875	PCSW	763712	PMS	794719	PCSE	892757	RMS	992353	PCE
708633	PME	745545	PCS	763973	PMSE	797133	PMW	894139	PCSE	992368	PC*

TQ	TR	TR	TR	TR	TR
993370	000382 PC-	094353 DMW	218587 PCSE	268385 SCSW	315409 SME
994189 SCS	001333	098295 PMSE	218673 PCNE	269385 PMS	315439
994321 PCS	001335	099015 RCS	222683 PMNE	269556 PMSE	316586
994352	001402 PCSE	101352 A/TB ×120	223493	273525	317412 SME
995354 PCE	002329	101617 PCS	224383 PCSE	274549 PMNE	318430 PCNW
996188 SCS	003325	102317 PCS	224570 PM-	275506	320410 PCSE
996982 PCE ×2	003404 PC★	104044 PCN	224578 PCN	279544 PC★	321430
997322 RCS	003957 RCS	106646 PME	225380 PCNW	280390	322442
997385 PCN	004334	107355 PCW	226382 PCS	281661 PCN	325427 ×6
998332 PCN	004608 DMSE	112342 PCS	226546 RMS	283403 SCSE	326439
999384 PC★	005393 PCS	128342	226563 PMW	283548 PM-	327438
999956 RCS	006393 PCN	129320 RMS	226582	283551 PMNE	327439
999965 PCE	005400 PC★	129323 PCSE	227570 PCE	285390	329528
	006386 PC-	133328	228358 PCS	286406 PCS	333436
	007383 PCE	138333 PCSE	228377 PCS	288537 PM-	333654 PCS
	007388 PCSW	138341	228382 PCSW	289583	334431 PMNW
	008381 PCSE	138655 A/TC	228544 PM-	290393	336421 PCSE
	009385 PCE	144604 PCN	228545 DM-	290403 SMSE	336472
	009391 PCSE	154348	230359 PCS	290439	337423
	012956 RCS	155657 PCNW	230381 PCS	291393	338433
	014966 PCSE	158339	232566	292399 SMNW	338531
	015330 PCS	188371 PCS	232676 PCN	294391	339424 RC
	018958 RCS	191354 PCNW	234739 PCS	294399 SMSE	339629 PCNE
	019957 PCSE	191381 PC	235359 PM-	296401 SMNW	339632 PCE
	020957 PCE	192349 PCS	235539 PME	296432	340423 CCSE
	022964 RCSE	192362 PCW	237377 PCS	297432	342424 CCSE
	025718 ★	192365 PCS	239378 PCS	298486	342425 PCSE
	026162 RCNE	193360 PCW	239534 PMNW	300410 SME	343430
	026964 RCNW	198383 PCN	239573	300504	344473
	027013 RMS	200357 PCS	240377 RC-	301401 PCSE	344636 PCSE
	027335 PCE	200551 PMSW	241374 PCSE	301403 SME	345428
	027963 RCSE	202365 PC★	241379 PC-	301490	345473 PCNE
	028332 A/TB ×3	202548 PMSW	241526	302403 RCSE	345479
	037338	203391 PMSW	242378 PCSE	302409 SME	347427
	048342	204354 PCSE	242379 RCSE	302411 SME	347460
	053677 PMSE	205392 PCNE	248581	303403 SMNW	347576
	054682 PCE	207381 PCS	249383 RCSE ×3	303504 PCSE	349426 ★
	055639 PMNE	207393 P/H	251502 A/TB	304404 SMNW	352427 RMSE
	055678 RCSE	208389 PMN	253568 PME	304406 SMSE	352428 RMSE
	059344 PCS	208395	253646 PCN	305403 SMN	352643
	061647 A/TB ×5	208397 PCN	254385 SCS	305404 SMW	353424
	063277 PCSW	209353 PCS	256471 PMSE★	306406 SMNW	353428 RMSE
	063282 PCW★	209396	256568 PMNE	306407 SMNW	355432 RCSE
	064283 PCN	210390 PCNE	257473 PMSE★	306427	355433 RCSE
	065283 PCNE	210399	257481	308403 SMS	355449
	066166	210595 PCE	258469 PMSE★	309403 SMSW	356429
	066279 PCSE	211374	258646 RMS	310409 SMNE	356458
	069342 PCS	211395 P/H	259646 RMS	311407 SMNE	356486
	075643 SC-	212373 PCSW	259651 RCNW	311408 SMNE	356542
	078343	212376 PC	261673 PCN	312403 SME	357436 PCSE
	078593 PMNE	212388 PMSE★	262466 PCS	312404 SME	357448
	079595 PCNE	213377 PCS	262561 PC-	312405 SMSE	357484 PCSE
	083272 PCSE	214393 PCNW	264465 PMSE	312406 SMNE	358436 RCSE
	084275 PCSE	215391 PCNW	265463 PCS	312555 PMSE	358452
	085207	216396 PCN	265464 PMSE	313403 SMSE	358651 PCNW
	085277 PCSE	216624 PCNE	267385 PMSE	314407 SMSE	359434 RCSE
	094344 PCS	217391 P/H	267673 PCN	314410 RCNE	359438 RCSE

83

TR	SM	SN	SO	SO	SP
359684 PM-	815036 RCS	057037 PMS	007333 PMNE	895415 RMN	045846
360433 RCSE	867019 DM-	063026 PMEW	031512 DCW	901963	065477 PMSE
360693	933170 PCNW	117001 PMSE	330093	918213 SCW	182040 PCS
362577	938066 RCNW	177459 PCS	371013 ×2	922423 RCSE	249000 PCS
363446	945327 RCE	247497 RM-	413868	924424 A/TC	252127 PCN
363656 PCS	958072 RCN★	250492 PM-	513127 RMSW	974258 PC★	298002 PMS
363679 PME★	961157 PM-	251497 RM-	518380 PCW	989879 PCS	298057 CC36
366457 PCSE	965158 PCE	252493 PM-	537011 ★		311004 PCSE
367441 RMSE	966159 PCN	253498 PM-	537378 RME		316060 A/W
368443	968068 RCNW	254494 PM-	567182 PMNE		317006 PCSE
369446 SMSE	988353 RCNE	244497 PM-	578191 LME		329002 PCSE
371552 PCSW	989023 PMSW★	255497 PM-	578192 LME		358005 PCSE
371554		356401 PCN	691046 RCNE		384018 PCS
375544		356401 PCS	693108 PCW		397014 PCS
376502 PMNE		367342 PME ×2	693113 PCN		402016 RMS
376692		373295	699119 PCNW		403016 RMS
378502 PCN		373483 PCS	701122 SCNW		406015 PCW
378511 CCE★		373495 PMW	702125 PCNW		413013 m.g.
378514 CCE		375188 RMEW	706126 SCN		415012 PCSW
379477 SMNE		383182 PCSW★	707110 A/TB		418005 RCN
379479 PME		389393	708130 PCN★		418006 RCSW
380486		393085 PMS	708983 PMW		419010 A/TP
		400047 RMNW	709043 PCNW		432648 PCNW
		404544 PCS	713047 PCW		455733
		405005 PCS	713126 PCNE★		482157 PCW
		405048 RMNW	714123 PCNE★		483182 RCNW
		405192 PMNW	716659 PMNW		484141 PCW
		407068 DMN	719050 PCNW		484141 PCN
		409018 PCS	720055 PCNW		485157 PCNE
		411050	745085		489108 PCW
		412016 PCS	752102 PCN		492103 RCNW
		415005 RC-×2	753097 PCW★		494104 SMS
		417005 PCSW	575095 RCNE		495290 PCSW
		418008 PCNE	765084 SCNE		496291 PCNW
		419002 PCSE	769070 PCSE		505105 PCN
		438057 PCSW	771073 PCSE		615483 PCNW
		472413 PMS	772075 PCNE		832682 DME
		580477 PCNE	773080 PCW		904952 PMN
		580807	781056 PMNE		919144
		580810 RMW	783061		920140
		581813 PCNE	794053		
		613897 PMSW	805220 PMNW		
		785101 PCSE	806195 PMSE		
		979633 PMSW	806224 PMN		
		988199 PMS×2	831087 A/TC		
		996329 PMSW	875151 PMW		
		999336 PMNW	877225 RM-		
			879149 DME		
			879223 ★		
			880217 PC-		
			882224 ★		
			887212 PM-		
			887223 PMS★		
			892154 PMW★		
			892222 PC36		
			893213		
			894222 PM36		

TL	TL	TL	TL	TL	TL
072473 PMSW	334045 PMN	456180 PMW*	494638 PMSE	542337 PCNE	587265 RMW
075483 PM36	334885 PME	456457 SMSE	495045 CC36	543337 RCNE	582276 PME
079463 PMW	337046 PMN	458179 PMSW	495220 PMNE	544334 PCSE	582277 smb
086002 DCN	339045 PMN	460188 PMNE	495444 RCE	545337 PME	582277 A/TB & C
089196 PMS	342044 PMN	460188 PMSE	495446 PCE	545337 A/TB ×15	583822 *
103024 PMNW	342044 A/TB	461860 PMN*	495640 PCE	546360 PCNW	583865
109017 PMW	343677	462185 PMN	496361 PMN	548959 PME	584274 PME
109019 PMN	344044 PMN	464495 PC36	497442 RCE	550330 PMN	584872
109021 PMW*	344890 A/TB	464517 PCS	498440 PCE	550599 m.g.	586269 PMSW
111022 PMN	344910 PME	465497 PCE	500649 PCS	551319 PME	587271 PME
112017 PMNE	347045 PMN	466493 RCE	501720 RCNE	551323 PME	588837 *
113014 *	349045 A/TB	466597	503213 PMNE	551319 PME	591272 PME
114013 *	349912 PME	467492 RCE	503658 PCE*	551327 PME	594270 RMNE
114015 PMNE	350972 PMNE	467502 PCE	504425 RCE	551807 PMSE	595263 PMS
117006 PMN	352045 PMN	467549 PCSE	504460 PMSE	553873	595270 PMN
129035 PCN*	352871 PMNE	469490 RMS	507003 RM-	555346	597435 PCNW
143021 PMN	355045 PMN	470592 RCSE	509424 RCE	555858	600267 PMN
158023 PCNW*	355131 PMSW	470593 PCE	511660 PCE	556311 PMN	600828 RCE
158048 DM-	357913 PMSE	471491 PC36	513259 PCN	557561 SC-	601256 PME
172994 PM-	357913 PMNS	473528 PCSE	513419 RCE	561310 PMN	601266 smb
175483 PMNE	359046 PMN	474311 PME	514260 PCN	561342 PMS	602253 RME
218085 DCS*	362052 PMN	474501 PC-	514371 PCN	562306 PMNE	603266 RMN
228133	369008 PCNW	475603 PCS	514417 PCE	564304 PMNE	603831 L/H
229493 PM-	369052 PMN	476487 PC36	515257 DME	564343 PMSE	604249 PMNE
243712 PMS	373019 PMNE	477219 PMW	515415 RCE	564355 PMNW*	604868 PCNE
243713 PCNE	373991 PCW	478485 RCE	516409 PCE	566354 PME	607241 *
245024 PMSE	374053 PCN	480479 PC36	518356 PCE	567301 RCSE	607246 PME
246713 PMSE	374069 L/H	482210 PMSE	518394 PCE	567344 PCS	607247 PME
246972 PCNW	375058	482474 PC36	519356 RC36	568303 PMSE	609245 PME
249011 PC-	376026 A/W	482482 PCE	519366 PCN	568305 RMNE	610233 PMSE
251129 CM36	376050 DCN	483045 PMS	519393	568296	609919 RMN
253993 PME	392056 PCNW	483463 PCE	519404 PCE	569814 PCE	610831
262968 PMNE	392056 A/TB ×12	484369 RME	520345 PCW	570290	611240 PMN
265990 PMNE	394012 PMS	485472 RCE	520349 PCNE	570293 RCSW	614935 RC-
267997 PME	397055 PCNE	486472 PCE	520358 CC36	570304	616239 PMN
274996 PMSE	398055 PCNE	486679 PM-	520361 RME	570869 RMN	617237 PCNE
275963 PMNE	399053 PCNE	487037 CC36	520364 PCE	571281	617823 PME
275993 PMNE	401052 A/TB ×6	487473 PCE	520368 RME	572287	618413 PCNE
277039 PMNE	406051 A/TB ×36	487477 PCE	521369 RMS	572349 PMNE	619236 PME
277039 A/TB	408050 PCS*	488452 PC36	521381 PCN	573288	619817 PME
287963 PM-	409646	488456 RCE	521381 A/TB	573614 PCNW	620237 RCN
288957 PM-	410050 PC*	488622 PCSE	521390 PCNE	573868	621236 PCNE
293939 A/TB	413052 A/W	491195 PMS	521390 PCSE	574308	621988 m.g.
298042 PMN	414070 L/H	491453 PCE	521390 A/TB ×2	575285 RME	622235 SCNE
298042 A/TB	417136 PMSE	492226 PMN	522345 PCW	575848 PME	622805 RCE
308047 A/TB	418045 PCE	492445 PC36	522372 PCE	575866	623804 PME
319708 PMN	418135 PMSW	492596 PMNW	523344 RMNE	576281 RME	624234 SCNE
325050 PMN	418651 PCS	492666 PMW	523614 PMSE	576863 *	625232 SCNE
326049 PMN	424979 PMNE	493051 PME	524341 PMNE	576877 smb	626233 SCE
329049 PMN	425267	493634 PME	528340 PMN	578818 PCE	627233 PCE
329049 A/TB	427974 PME	494046 PMN	532340 PMN	578864	628228 SCE
329915 PMW	433633 PCE	494047 PCE	533622 PCNW	579882 smb	628231 SCE
331051 PMN	434570 PCSW	494048 PME	535725 PCW	580877 *	629223 PCNE
331912 PMS	435581 PM-	494049 PCE	535854	581874 RMN	630226 PCE
332047 PMN	435598 PMW	494051 PCN	537339 PCNW	583268 PME	634218 PCE
333675 PCE	454183 PMW	494193 PMS	537715 PCE	584265 RMS	635211 RCSE
	454459 PCNW	494448 PCE	541336 RCN	587848	635218 SCE

TL	TL	TL	TL	TL	TL
636209 PCSE	696162	737063 PMSE	772726 PME	875812 PCN	910535 smb
636213	696166 PCNE	738031	776718 PME	877610 PCE	910765 PCE
636214	697157 RCNE	738074 PCE	780714 PMNE	878408	912518 PC-
636215 PCNE	698147 RCNE	739076 PCE	783775 PCS	879606 PCE	912530 PC-
636217	700136 PME	740028 PMSE	783775 smb	880384 PME	914498 PCS
637212 PCSE	700138 A/TB ×2	740028 PCSE	786709	880385 PME	914750 PCE
637213 PCE	700145 RCSE	740034 RCS	786776 PCS	880387 PME	916499 SCS
637217 SCE	700740 PMN	741035 PCS	787866 ★	881381 PME	916517 PCE
637780	701135 PME	741046 RCS	789188 PCN	881403 ×4	918505 PME
638206 PCNE	702904 m.g.	741049 PCNE	789709 PMNE	881413 DM36	918725 PMSE
638630 PCW	703132 PMSE	741056	794971 PCSW	882473 PMSE	919501 PC-
640768	704126 PCN	741059 RCE	797711 PMNE	883379 PME	920267
641205	704137 PCNE	741062 RCS	802709 PMNE	883475 PMSE	922405 PCE
645205	705128 PMNE	741075 SCNE	811705 PMNE	884598 PCE	921533 PCE
648204	705128 RCSE	741076 PCNE	814803 PCSW	885479 PMSE	922528 PCE
648658 PCS	706123 PCE	741078 PCNE	817703 PMNE	887376 PME	928272
649763 RCNE	706124 PME	742027 RCS	822155 PC-	887595 PCE	948688 PCE
650204	706129 RCSE	742032 PCE	830691 PME	888371 PME	951685
652199	707126 RME	742035 RCE	833651 PCN	888586 PCE	952681
652202	707739 PMNW	742036 RCE	833685	889005 PME	953675 PCW
654656 PCN	708127 RCE	742038 RCS	835682 PMNE	889594 PCNE	954674
661201	709125 RCNE	742041 RCSE	845992 PMNW	889813 PCSW	954679
660658 PMN	709126 PCE	742043 RCE	848994 PMNE	891596 PCNE	965259
660756 RCNE	709739 PMSW	742046 RCS	852660 PCNE	894801 PCSE	967096
660761 PMNE	710123 RCNE	742053 RCNE	854442	895285	969257 PC-
665212 smb	710743 PMW	742063 SCE	855438	895364 PME	973090 RCS
666202	711115 RCE	742069 PCSE	857434	895367 PME	973255 PCN
669200 ★	711122 RCE	742073 DCE	857444	895488 PCSE	976256 PCN
671751	712113 RCNE	745023 PCE	858429	895797 PCE	981097 PCSE
672176	712114 PCE	745026 RCN	860428	896355 PME	982253
672184 ★	712119 PCSE	743057 PCSE	860446 PME	896558	987104 PCE
674174	713101 RCN	743074 PCNE	863423 PMNE	897488 RCSE	991625 PCN
674408 PCNW	713104 DME	744053 PCNE	863426	897490 PC36	992223 PCS
675177	714091 PCSE	744076 PCE	863637 PCE	897556	992228 PMS
676173	714094 PCE	743635 RCE	863798	897782 PCSE	992265 ★
676180	714099 SCS	745015 PCW	864195 PCS	898353 PCNE	994228 PMS
676746 PCN	714101 SCNE	745865	864634 RCE	898554 PCE	994264 PCW★
677748 PMNW	715111 PCNE	745023 PME	864801 PC-	900372 RCW	994763
679746 RMNW	716743 PCS	746024 PMNE	865409 DMS	900470 RCN	
680414	717008 SCNE	747008 PME	866412	900491 RCSE	
682171	720743 PCN	747013 PCE	867420	901545 PCE★	
684170	722295 PMNW	746021 RCN	867627 PCE	902549	
684172	723083	747024 RCSE	867831 DMNE	903541 PCE	
685746 PMN	723086 ★	747025 PCSE	868408	903867 PCNW	
687169 PCNE	723387	749001 PCNE	868415	904309 PMNE	
688171 PCNE	723725 PMN	750005 PCE	868419	904347 PME	
689743 PCN	725083 SCNE	751005 PCNE	868625 PCE	904351 PME	
690172 RMNW	727082 SCNE	754001 PMW	868837 PCN	904493	
690173 RCNE	727738 RMNW	754001 RMNW	869622 PCE	905312 PMNE	
692741 PCN	729084 SCNE★	754001 RMN	871140 PCE	905340	
693164 PCNE	730086 A/TB ×2	754001 RME	871825 DM-	905348 PME	
693170	732079 SCSE	756000 RME	872615 PCE	905541 PCE	
695160	734083 SCE	756725 PCN	872824 ★	906345 PMNE	
695165 RME	735281	759722 PCN	873614 PCW	907538 PCE	
696139 PCNE	735865 PMW	759727 PCN	873851 PCN	908498 PCE	
696150 RCE	736080 SCE	771725 PME	875407	910496 PCSE	
696155 PCSE	736083 SCE		875846 PCSE	910523	

TM	TM	TM	TM	TM	TM
001258	073154 PMSE	240277 PCE★	308467 RMNW	413716 RM36	494752 RMN
003259 RMN	073533	243326 ★	311003 RMS	415596 RCSE ×2	494767 SNE
004224 PCS	077616 SCSE	243776 PMSE	313585 PMNE	416597	496744 RMW
004261 PME	083157 Martello	244302 PCSW	314785	417593 RCSE	496744 RME
005092 RCN	092150 RCS	245811 PMN	316444 CCW	421910 PMW	496744 PMS
006088 PCN	092867 PM-	247297 ×2	317366	422886 PCS	499745 A/TB ×90
006229 RCW	099326 RME	247446 PMS	318817 PME	426906 PMN	499773 RM36
006253 RCNW★	105264 RM36	247465 RC36	319792 PM-	428932 PMSE	500745 A/TB ×20
007257 RMN	109127 PCS	248317 SCN	322580 PMNW	434908 PME	501902 PCE
009225 A/TP	109805	249445 PMSE	325777 PM-	437676 PCNE	503760
009248	110125 PCE	249460 PMNE	330900 PCW	437893 PMNE	503761
010093 RCN	114808	250445 PMSE	332382	444596 SCS	504769 CCN
013152 PMSE	118127 PCS	251457 RC36	336887 PMS	444867 PCE	504828 RM-
013249 RCN	119124 PCS★	252317 PCSE	337780 PCN	446596 SCN	505760
014152 PMSE	123438 PCN	253310 PCE	338900 PCE	447595 SCN	505768 PMNE★
014153 PCSE	124438 PCSE	255321 SCS	338902 PCN	448596 SCN	507777 PM36
014229 PME	127125 PCS★	256795 PMN	345407 CCE	452991 PME	508756
015249	127127 PCS	257314 SCN	345424 CCW	453591 LCE	509758
016230 A/TP	127794 PMS	258316 PCN	345425 CCE	455779 RC36	509902 PCE
016429 PCE	127796 PCE	258325 PCN	346408 PCW	455796 Aux	511770 A/TB ×60
020095 RCN	131127 PCS★	258327 PCN	347388 PMSE	456590 LCE	511844 PME
020095 RCS	142874	259316 PCN	347416 PCE	456746 PCNE ×2	512766
020123 PM★	146444 PME	261317 PCNW	351391 CCE	456765 PME	512772
020123 DEL	148734 PMSE	261317 PCN	353394 PCSE	456777 PMSW	512921 PMN
022087 PCN	151429 PCW	261318 PCNE	354416 PME	456994 PCNE	513775 A/W
022423 PCE	153465 PMSE	262317 DCW	355396 PCE	460983 RME	513845 RCE
025086 PCNE	158424	262318 DCW	355397 RCE	460985 PME	520804 PME
025093 RCNE	158707	262319 DCW	356398 Martello	461561 SMSE	522800 RM36
026822 PM-	160423	262320 PCW	356423 PCE	464681	522948 PCW
029079 PCE	164470 PMSE	262326 SCW	358401 CCE	464790 PCE	523938 ★
029083 PCNE	169436 RCE	263317 DCE	358401 RCE	465682 DCW ×2	523949 PCNW
029089 RCNE	169473 ★	263317 SCN	358402 PCE	465875 PMS	524944 A/TB ×4
029165 RCSE	175473 PMSE	266236 PCE	358402 SCE	469612 RMSE	524950 PCW
031087 RCN	175473 PMNE	266239 PCNE	359423 PCE	470613 RME	525822 RME
031087 RCE	176820 PM-	267238 PCE	359601	471595 A/B ×6	525929 PMNW
032078 RCE	185248 PCW	267774 PMNW	359777 PC-	472610 PMSE	525931 PCNW
032126 PCS	197863 L/H	269829 DMW	360420 PCE	472627 RME	525951 PCW
033214 RCNE	212180 SMSE	272724	360990 PMNW	473660 RME	525954 A/TB ×85
036167 RCSE	213293 PCW	273813 PMNE	361420 Martello	473660 A/TB ×100	526813
041130 ★	220174 PCSE	275718 RC-	362423 PCE	474968 PMS	526929 PCN
041168 RCSE	222175 PCSE	277717	365978 PCS	475626 RMSE	526954 A/TB ×2
041212 RCNE	224918	280756 PC-	366426 Martello	476601 PME	527933 PCSW
047667	225177 RCSE	280816	366439 PCSE	476631 A/TB ×6	528540 PCE
048769	225178 PCSE	281671 PME	366921 PMNE	476634 A/TB ×40	528896 A/W
049762	225308 PCW	281698 PC-	367439 CCSE	476637 A/TB ×40	529859 RM36
050871 PM-	226627 RCNE	282315 PC36	367441 CCS	476642 A/TB ×40	529862 PMSE
051168 RCSE	226313 PCW	283313 PCSE	369440 SCS	477708 A/TB	530867 RME
052170 RCNE	228630 RCNE	283313 RCSE	369441 SCS	478707 RCNE ×2	531962 PCN
056138 SCSE	229182 PCSE	283350	371440	480700 A/TB ×400	532826
057138 RCS	230313 PCW	283857 PMNW	372978 PCE	487740 RMS	532835 RM-
058163 RCSE	234316 SCW	284856 PME	373821 PM-	487907 PME	532926
059166 RCNE	235204	285671 PCNE	375633 PM-	490740 PMS	532958 PCNE
067147 PCSE	235228 PCN	289983 RMN	378631 PM-	490744 RMS	534835 RM-
069148 PCSE	235237 A/TB	297613 PMNW	388779	490875 PMSE	534837 RM-
069817	237312 PCS	297805 PM-	392769 PMSW	491867 PCNE	534840 RM-
072150 PCS	238312 SMN	300803	393767 PMSE	491869 PCNE	534944 A/TB ×90
072534	239275 PCE★	301799	394969 PM-	492868 PCNE	534946 PCS

TM		SH		SH		SJ		SJ		SK	
534953	PCW	234801	*	781806	DMW*	143591	PCSE	918829		019213	
534954	PC-	235838	PCSE*	835368	SCS	185469	PCS	926655	PCE	046177	PCSW
534959	PCNW	237837	RM			196516	PCNW	931637	PMS	055694	DM-
535875	RME	240840	PCE			237856		941605	PMNE	061690	DM-
535952	PCW	250802	*			240735	RMW ×2	941605	PMSE	071427	
535960	PCN	251822	CMS			284779		945225		072749	
536838	A/TB ×16	252793	CCSE			303827		975216		080427	RM-
536849	SME	252796	CMSW			343842	PCW			081689	OP
536855	RME	252827	CMNW*			343842	PCE			104400	RC-
536868	RME	253834	m.g.			370784	SM-			105345	PC ×2
536881	RME	254791	CMSE			371783	SM-			111399	RC-
536949	PCW	256793	CMSE			373504	DMNW			118318	PCN
537837	*	256798	CMSW			382487	RM36			120432	PC ×2
537885	RME	260823	RCSE			383489	RM36			127314	PCN
537970	A/TB ×30	261794	CMSE			383490	RM36			132178	
538839	A/TB ×100	261805	CMSE			383495	RM36			134318	PCN
538943	PC*	262822	CCN			384492	RM36			141315	PCN
538960	PMN	266818	DMNW			385483	SM36			148318	PCN
538962	PCNW	268802	CCE			385485	RM36			159460	RCS
539944	PC*	269795	CME			387486	SM36			181161	PC-
539989	SMSE	270802				387488	RM36			268268	PC-
540962	PMN	274808				387491	RM36			273271	PCE
541954	SCE	275803				387654				311331	PMSE
541955	SCE	341334	RMS			389486	SM36			338461	×2
542985	PCSE	374939	PCW			389487	RM36			445264	
544963	PCN	432579	SMW			389490	RM36			504403	PCS
545959	SCN	433577	SMW			389492	RM36			534804	PME
545962	SCN	433583	PMS			391489	RM36			572357	
547964	A/TB ×36	435572	SMW			391491	RM36			573545	
547964	SCE	436565	DCNW			395676	SM36			584307	
548951	SCE	441584	SM ×3			413855	PCS			590441	
548961	SCE	565235	*			453670	RM36			605468	
549954	SCE	574514	RCN			539095	PME			675304	SMNE
549954	CMW	575220				540094	PME			739455	PM-
549955	m.g.	579305	DMNW			556659	SMSW			785057	
549956	SCE	580212	RMW*			558216	PMNE			788058	
549957	SCE	580808	RCW			593047	PMSE			790359	PMSE ×2
549958	SCE	581092	RMW			594044	PMNW			791247	
549959	SCE	582813	PCS			596050	PMN			822317	PCN
549961	RCE	584377	PCW			612178	RMSE			840151	PMSW
550959	SCE	593195	RMW			629995	RM-			875905	
553927	PME	593474	smb			632998	DM-			888628	PMSW
		606731				668985	RME			897052	
		610104	A/TB			670984	CM-			913002	PMSW
		612121	PCW			684346	PC36			926214	PCNW
		612124	PMW			702019	SMNW			928208	PCW
		617665	SCSE			718184	PCNE			951352	PMSW
		646606	DMSW			790243	PCS			965200	PCS
		648604	smb ×3			875895	PMS			972215	
		655605	DMS			892830				988250	PCW
		657558	RMW			893817				990355	PMS ×2
		659557	RMW			896875	PM-			995060	
		662558	PME			899807	SM36				
		662560	RME			903662	PCS				
		703702	PCS			911709	PCSE				
		773674				915822					
		781805	DMW*			918819					

TF	TF	TF	TF	TF	TG
007612 PCSW	334430 PCE	483883	565603 PCE	888069 PCN	003255 PME
024012	335430 SME	484211 PCNE	566587 PCE	891444 SCNE	005202 PMN
039563 PCSE	339468 RCS	485786	566594 PCSE	893442 SCE	014416 PMN
047562 PCS	351517 RMNW	486879	566703	895439 A/W	020326 PMN
050574 PMN	359403 SCW	488854	568622 RCE	899358	027331 PM*
133780 DC36	360402 PCW	489882 RCNE	568699	906374 PMW	029451 A/W*
175357 PC-	361401 PCW	491846	571642 RCE	906376 PMNE	033365 PMNE
203063 *	365399 A/TB ×16	492206 PMN	572644 RCE	909375 PME	033372
214062	365400 PCNE	493206 PMS	572645 RCE	913443 PMS	036272
216071 PMNE	367416 RC36	493870	572646 RCE	914441 PCN	044426 PMN
218061 A/TB	373505 PCN	496587 *	572647 RCE	925011	047443 A/W
219068 PME	394411 PCSE	496829	573634 PCE	928214	050453 PMS
219072 PMNE	396413 PME ×2	497857	573639 DCE	935269 PCE	052441 PMNE
221079 PME	396417 PCE	498002 SMNE	574687 PCSE	941365 PCE	055452
227046	396420 RCE	498849	575012 PMN	955215 PMNE	061441 m.g.
233057 *	397424 PCE	498869	577014 SMN	975423 PMW	063955
237054 PCSE	398030	501792	582015 SMN	972426 PMNE	070439 PMN
245238 RCN	406436 RCE	501838	590241 SCN	975360 PMS	071431 A/W
247057 SMN	407440 RCE	502613 *	602200 A/TB ×4	985369 PMN	072439 PMN
250049 PMN	408338 PCNE	503821	617195 CCN*	989538 PC-	072439 A/TB
250054 PMN	410339 RCE	505807	618008 PCE	993162 PM-	077444 RMEW
250055 A/TB ×4	413445 RCE	511797	626187 A/TB	993540 PC-	079444 smb
261053 PMN	415450 PCSE	513833	663367 SCW	994132 PM-	084442 smb
262047 PMN	421999 RCNE	515840	663368 SCW	994260 PMN	087442 PMN
265539 PCSE	422002 RME	519827	672199 PMS	994544 PC-	089172 PMSW
267047 PMN	423002 PMN	523821	681306 PCW	997547 PC-	089269 PCSW
267052 PMN	425999 RCE	533157	681426 PMN*		092441 PMN
267110	434471 PCE	536723	688426 PMN		093439 CCN
267475 PMNW	435474 PCE	536797	688432 PMNW		096440 PMNW
271016 PMNE	442968 A/TC ×10	738745	690061 PC-		098441
271021 PMNE	443962 RCNE	539788	691064 PMN		100425 PCN
272004 PMN	445958 RCE ×2	541625	694440		102182 m.g.
272030 PMN	445958 A/TC ×10	546773	695262		102415 PMS
273014 PMS	448953 RCE	549690	699435 RMW		103157
273028 PME	450952 RCNE	553582 PCE	714312		103438 PMN
273051 PMN	455094 L/H	553673	728108 PMS		111437 PCNW
274002 PME	455933 RCSW	554014 RMNW	742164 PMN		111438 PCN
274040 PMSE	456935 RCS	554695	744066 PM-		112272 PMSE
276009 PME	456944 PCSE	554753	755406 PMN		114304 PMN
276023 PME	460520 PCN	556015 PMNW	764144 A/TR ×36		115436 PMN
277043 PMSE	460528 *	556579 A/TB ×13	770452 RCW		116428
278019 PMNE	460932 PCE	556582 PCS	771445 RCN		116432 PMN
279049 RMNE	460933 PCSE	557582 PCSE	771452 RMN ×2		118420
280046 PME	462928 RCE	558578 RCSE	773223 PMS		119414
280047 PME	464925 PCE	558743	782394		120436 smb
282043 RME*	465816	559012 PMN	787397 PMNE		122214 PM-
286352 RC36	465923 RCNE	561577 PCSE	814084 PMSE		123431 PCN
300557 RCE	465924 A/TB ×11	562578 PCSE	815095 PCNE		124432 PCN
312105	465924 A/TC ×5	562580 A/TS	818018		126436 SMN
312445 RME	467801	563732 PCE	820325 PMN		125433 PMN
312529 RCSE	468917 RCE	564708	826421		127435 PMN
318323	475286 RCE	564715	827419 SMN		128214 PMNE
327432 RCS	478872	564720	873440 A/TB		128436 smb
327433 RCS	478901 RCE	565606 PCE	880442 SCN		132426
327435 RCSW	479886	565011 PMN	881443 SCN		133426 A/W
328472 SCN	480884	565593 RCSE	883248 PMN ×2		133433
329435 RCSW	483269 RCSE	565594 DMSE	886247 PME		135428

TG		TG		TG		TG		SC		SD	
139138	RME	264196	PCN	360233	CM36	503005	A/TB ×4	360979	PMNE	048994	
140390	SC-	264199	PMNE	360321	PCNW	504086	PM-	365994	PCSW	048985	DMW
140410		265220		364314	PCE	504087	PM-	453975	RCE	055970	DMW
140413		268078	PMS	367317	PCE	504090	PCN			078996	PM-
141391	PMNE	268223		368314	SMNE	504185	PCN			113868	CC-
142276	DMS	272215	PM-	373172	DMSE	505093				173695	RCW
142346	PMSE	272015	RMNE	373172	smb	512165	PCE			175691	RCN
143390	PMN	272311	PMNE	374315	PMSW	507173	A/TB ×32			182678	RCS
147436	⋆	272334	CM36	375317	PMSW	508174	DCNS			182679	RCE
148348	PM-	272348	Aux	376317	PCE⋆	509169	PMNE			187677	PCSE
151278	PCNE	273230	PMNE	380312		509169	A/TB ×40			188678	PCSE
154431	A/TB ×6	279218	CCSE	385306	PCE	510005	A/TB ×3			189687	
156431	A/TB	279318	PMNE	387305	SCE	513068	DMSE			189691	PCNW
159423	RCN	274212	PMN	388175	PMS	513156				189701	PCN
163126	RMS	275088	A/TB ×47	392302	PCNE	513161	PMNE			189712	RCW
166413	RMN	281218	CCSE	394071	PME	513161	smb			189721	RCW
167422	⋆	285317	CCN	396116	PM-	515008	smb			191727	RCW
169433		288382	PME	397200		515068	PM-			194680	PCSW
171233	PCSE	290385	PME	398112	PMN	515124	PCNE			195677	PCW
171428	PMW	295382	PCS	398298	PCSE	515147	PMW			195678	PCW
178343	PME	296168	PMS	400293	PMNE	516125	PCNE			196517	
181432		296313	PME	402189	SCE	517083	PM ×2			196676	PCW
183405	CCE	296378	PCS	402105	DMSE	517068	PM-			197673	PCSW
191320	RME	297314	CCNE ×2	404288	PCSW	518065	PCW			197675	PCW
195264	PMS	298308	CCNE	407106	PME	518073				199672	PCSW
196264	PMSE	300307	DMNE	407280	PME	518125				200671	PCS
197275	DCE	302830	PMN	410100	PME	519009	PMSE			202670	PCS
205114	PMNW	305359		411107	PMSE	519064	PCW			203671	
205114	A/TB	307298	CC36	412290		519127	PCW			203681	SME ×2
205377	CCE⋆	307363		413284	PCNE	520053	PMSE			204677	PCSW
205427	PME	308295	CC36	413289		520079	PMSW			205681	PCS
207421	RMNW	310299	PME	420184	CCS	521095	PMSW			205683	PCE
208421	RMSW	313275	PMNE	421281		521135	PMW			206679	PCS
209421	LMNE	314276	PMNE	422269	CCE	521145	PME			207676	PCS
210420	PMW	315365		423018	m.g.	521145	smb			210678	PCS
213132	PMNE	316275		424066	PMW	523136	PMSE			217685	PCS
213357	PC⋆	319022	PMSE	427070	PMS	524015	PMSE			218745	PCW
214420	PMSW	326371	PCE	428070	PME	525106	DCN			220682	PCS
216417		328268	PMNE	442090	DME	526011	PMSE			304023	PMW ×2
217219	PME	337339	PCNE	442264	PCE	527122	RCNE			308057	RCW
225239	PMNE	337342	RMS	454249	PMNE	530100	RMW			314067	SCW
227127	PMSE	337342	smb	461121	PME	532016	⋆			316080	SCW
227416	PMN	338260	SCNE	465241	PME	535002	⋆			327313	RMS
235408	PMN	338333	RMN	469202	RMN					330105	PCS
240078	CM36	340341	PCS	469238	RMS					330843	PCSW
240363	⋆	341332	PME	471022	PME					331315	PCNE
241353		345248	RME	483063	CCN					332314	PCN
242354		345337	PCE	485217	A/TB					339841	PCSE
242072	PMNW⋆	347246	PMNE	492209	PMNE					341843	PCSW
249024	PCW	349247	PMNE	496161						343083	SCW
252027	PCN	349249	CCNE	497090	PCNE					344842	PCW
253026	PCS	349318	PMNE	497172	PMS					347841	PCW⋆
261236	PCN	349337	LME	498008	A/TB ×5					449095	SMW
265236	PMSE	350323	PCSW	498197	A/TB ×80					351063	SCW
263121	PMNE	352058	RME	499178	PMSW					352063	PCE
263356	RCNW	355326	PCNE	500008	SCE					353063	SCW
264119		357983	PMSE	502175	PMNE					375202	PCE

SD		SE		TA		NX		NY		NZ	
382868	PCNW	018047	DME	016455		360005	RCNW	002794	PCE	013645	PCN
383204	PC★	129952	RCN	122783	RCE	840631	PMW	003791	PCN	045696	PCS
391114	PCNW★	130954	RCN	122788	RCE	846636	PMN	006787	PCE	048491	PCS
403829	PCS	397759	★	123784	SCE	988783	PCSW	007785	PCE	069699	PME
404832	PCS	398757	RCE	125781	PCE	989795	PCN	032366	A/W	070691	PMSE
408833	PCSW	509323		126775	SCE	991788	PCW	065297		079962	PCN
419801	RCSW	515322		126781	PCE	992794	PCN	079446		089664	
420805	PCS ×2	524329		136330		994796	PCN★	079447		090996	PCN
425810	PCSW	950260	PCE	169624	PCE	996783	PCS	082342		094667	
427812	PCSE	954586		169625	SCE	997796	PCS	084240		099995	PCN
432413				169626	RCE	999796	PCE	089389		108540	PCNW
446114				169627	SCE			122536	P/H	115651	PCN
460109	CCN			169628	SCE			138567	m.g.	115985	PCNE
460150	RMW			169629	SCW			140537		118651	
475110	CCN			173572	PCSE			144568	CCNW	127815	DCE
497851	PCW			173584	PCE			325255		127982	PCNE
498308	★			174563	PCSE			329107	PCS	131598	
499295				177559	PCSE			330101	PCE	133692	PCN
522646	A/TC			179550	PCE			331104	PCE	136355	PCS
525646	PCSW			179552	PCSE			353518		139984	PCN
570105	RC-			182545	PCSE			356648		143843	PCN
584696	PCW			193513	PCE			374689		152993	
584696	A/TC			194513	PCN			394646		159745	PCN
599016	PCNW			195507	PCE			395595		166991	
601355	PCE			196475	PCS			403531		168547	PCN
603018	RM-			196509	SME			403571	DME	169855	PCE
603787	PCS			198483	PCS			414659		172858	PCN
613785	PCS			207487	PCE			432526		176863	PCN
617781	PCSW			208472	PC-			473829	a.t.r.	177868	PCN
622316	PCN			232137	DEL			482827	a.t.r.	182997	
630780	PC-			242662				491497		192997	
636312	PCN			269091	RME			550404	m.g.	201858	DMNE
732365				298099	DCNE			566336	a.t.r.	202939	PCE
734152	PC-			351034	PCE			569619	DMSW	204925	PCSE
734365	PC-			354030	RC-			668218	PCSW	213865	PCN
782194	PCN-			355031	RCNE			702486		214865	PCN
785370	PC-			381019	OP			758083	PC-	228367	PCSE
801371	PC-			406007	A/TB ×30			767068	PMSW	236862	
812382	PC-			410007	m.g.			879125	PC-	241528	PCE
820410	PC-			413004	RC-			942895	PCN	273974	
825405	PC-			415005	RCE ×2			943895	PCNW	275972	
871115	PCS							950900	PCNW	275974	
883161	PCN							973990	PCN	276968	
903355	PCS							982261	m.g.	277125	PCS
940683	PCS							984999	PCN	278959	
										279957	
										280950	
										280952	
										280956	
										280968	
										281949	SME
										281951	
										281953	
										281955	
										282948	
										282950	
										282953	

NZ	NZ	NS	NT	NU	NU
283670 SCSE	488387 RCE★	355265 RC ×2	165842	001007 PCN	230281
283946	489278 A/TB ×17	355265 A/TB ×6	190826	006519	231224 PCW
283950	490277 RCSW	674714 ★	196785	007518	231279
291937	490281 RCNW	785978 m.g.	207805	008013	232282 RCS
291939	492279 RCSW	792986 m.g.	221766 PMN★	008515	233033 PCW
293127 RCS	492351 RCN	803967 RSN	229756 PMN★	009512	233265
293937	493272 RCSW		243770 SMN	024466 RCE	233285 RCS
299129 RCSE	493348 RCW		247736 PMW	033481	237260
301914	494346 RCSW		250667	035480	238042
301915	496275 RCSE		251669 SMNE	036012 PCN	242244
302855	496348 RCS		266862	045009 PCN	242233
302907	501287 RCNE		270863	053226 PCS	243228 SCN
303907	502363 RCW		276772 RMN★	056011 PCN	243233
303909	514264 RCNE		292956 PCN	059173 PCN	243235
308866	514264 A/AP		293828	059456	243253 PCE
309896	517321 RCE		450800 ★	061013 PCN	244221 RCE
310870	529291 RCNE		462827 A/TB	064427 PCW	244239 DCE
311895	530228 RCN		470831 A/TB	067004 PCN	244241 PCE
311826	531342 ★		557844 DCN	067428 PCE	244241 DCE
318880	535286 RCNE★		778000 PCN	068688	246225 PCE
318881	555258 SCN		956298 PCW	078216 PC-	247212 DCW
320881	556274 RCNE		978001 PCNE	080433 PCE ×2	247214 DCN
321799	557282 RCW		982278 PCNW	088123	248055
323785	558267 RCN		986277 PCSW	104195 PCNE	248099
325785	560213 SM-		986284 PCN	104346 PCN	248108
327349 PMN	562265 RCSW		988277 PCSE	105196 PCSE	249201 PCW
327782	568263 SC36		989285 PCE	105347 PCE	250090
334549	575254 RCN		993003 PCN	108193 PCSE	250107
334769	576254 RCNE			125093 m.g.	251085
335769	577254 RCNE			154309 PCE	252079
338550 PCN	578257 RCNE			159042 SMNE	253057
342758 PME	601219 RMN			162180 PCN	253076
346756 PME	603219 RCN			162358	253077
353754 PCS	606118			175361 PMNE	253078
368138 RCS	619127 RCW			178354 PCW	253223 PCE
374693	621225 RCSE			178355 PCE	254078
384667 LCE	621226 RCNW			178356 SCE	254198 PCW
396655 LCE	622229 RCNE			187352	254222
401255 A/TB ×2	650221 LCSE			191153 PCS	255064
403237 RCW	804054 DMS			192067 PCE	255071
404232 RCE				195122 L/H	256216 SCW
404238 RCE				198049	257116
408173 RCN				198339	258065
419132 PCS				198341	259049
434267				201341	259062
442430 CC-				202033	261145 PCE
442459 A/TB				203338	262125
445121 PCS				205336	262157
452324 PM36				208000	267040
466154 PCSW				208314 PCSE	275045
467152 RCS				210328	277005
468161 RCNE				213285 RCW	277006
478370 RCE				222016	278006
484336 RCW				226314	279009
485341 RCN				228273	279039
486343 RCE				228316	285031
487336 RCE				229279	287030
					288032

NO	NO	NH	NJ	NK	NC
159224 PCS	809884 PCN	521455 RMNE	012569 PM36	001658 PCNE	579058 RCE
159229 PMN	843884 PCN	579936 RCNE	013582	083339 PCE	582059 RCW
159229 A/TR	843884 A/TB	592920 RCE	017567 PMN	084335 PCE	584046 RCE
160268 PMNE	870873 PCN	606655 PCE	020572 PMN	086355 PCSE	612057 PCS
169253 PMNE	912969 PMNE	608914 RCN	022586 PMN	093358 PCNW	959098 OP
185224 A/TR		608918 RCNE	025587	121478 PCE	
2950933 SMSE		609915 RCE	033584 PMSW		
303030 PCE		645464 PCN	035593 PCN		
392314		702707 PM-	035647 A/TB		
439023 A/TB ×2		810687 OP	037647 PCNW		
468278 A/TB ×220		811670 OP	045645 A/TB		
471277 PCE		950615 A/AP ×200	045647		
472276 PCE			055645 PCN		
472277 A/TB ×600			057625 PMN		
478418 PCSE			065645		
486413 PCSE			070645		
467417 PCNE			077646		
495282 A/TB ×114			083647 PCN		
495419 PCNE			099654 PCN		
497225 A/TB ×589			114685 PCNW		
497225 A/TP ×210			228628		
498228 A/TB ×9			230623		
498228 Steel			238623		
499276 PCE			263686		
499276 PCNW			292451		
499276 A/TB ×35			308383		
500242 A-TB ×22			318424 PMN		
500276 A/TB ×272			326661		
500277 PCW			330399		
501260 OP			355131		
502179 A/TB ×324			392128 RCW		
502259 PCE			407488 PMSW		
502261 PCE			421509		
502261 A/TB ×28			511674 DMN		
502261 PCE			528060		
503248 ★			556664 PCN		
503322 ★			562663 PMN		
505172 Sea Wall			589665 DMN		
505989 PCW			643125 SCN		
524318			688647 DMN		
536988 PCN			785205		
538508 PCE			873135 PC-		
575151 PCNE			875116 PMS		
610376 A/TB ×49			878143 CMS		
652861 DCW ×2			890115 SCE		
688512 A/TB ×26			904033 PCW		
720594 PM-			926478		
721600 PME			957303 RMN		
721603 PCNE			980180 SCE		
723568 CCN					
725568 RMNE					
727568 RMNE					
729568 CCNE					
734622 A/TB ×50					
738621 A/TB ×50					
795991 RM-					
807881 PCN					

ND	HY	HU
374925 OP	420914 P/H*	340684 A/TB ×50
423937 CCSE	361140 RCE	483407 PCE
475982 SCN	448099 CCS	
479948 m.g.	471084 PCSW	
	472088 CCSE	
	473085 CCSE	
	539118 A/TP ×14	
	550040 A/TB ×200	
	551062 SCW	
	554062 SCW	

Uses of Pillboxes for other purposes

ALTHOUGH PILLBOXES DID NOT serve in their designed role in the UK, a number have been used for a variety of purposes that can be printed here.

Mrs Duff remembers when she was 'bombed out' at Lowestoft, the local soldiers took them to a pillbox on the corner of Pakefield Road, until more suitable accommodation could be found after the raid. Elizabeth Pettitt, who lived with her family at Deangate, Hoo, Kent, had a pillbox opposite her home. Her father fitted it up with a kitchen range, bunk beds and all mod. cons. and the family with friends used it regularly during the Blitz. Other pillboxes provided shelter from the elements for members of the Home Guard on duty, people waiting for a bus and children going home from school. Pillboxes were used as observation posts during the war and since by bird-watchers along the east coast. Disused pillboxes near Yarmouth have been reported as nest sites for Black Redstarts and no doubt other birds have found the loopholes satisfactory nesting places. They have housed tramps and others, some on a semi-permanent basis, the occupants having to be evicted before demolition could take place. During the war a crew who baled out from a Royal Air Force Wellington bomber, returning from a raid over Germany, landed on Wrangle Marsh, Lincolnshire. They hid in a pillbox, as they thought their landing had been in Holland. Today half a pillbox along the towpath of the Kennet and Avon Canal serves as a fishermen's shelter, while at Swanage other emplacements provide shelter for holidaymakers.

They have served as pigsties in Wiltshire, garden sheds, stores for builders, and one has found use as the base of an office in a boatyard. Larger varieties of pillboxes provide shelter for horses or cows and one of the hexagonal pattern was used to store petrol for the Bustard Flying Club at Old Sarum, while at the nearby Old Sarum rings the underground headquarters, once topped by a pillbox, is now the public toilets for this ancient monument.

Mr K. Richardson named his home at Ridlington, Norfolk, 'Pillbox Cottage', as everyone referred to it by that title, because of one sited in the corner of the garden. One or two have been incorporated into the garden scene, with climbing plants obscuring their hard outlines more effectively than their original camouflage.

An unlikely subject, but pillboxes have featured in poetry and, though not much has been written about them, much has been written on them!

Finally, pillboxes have been constructed around the world since 1945 in other countries, including Albania and Vietnam, where they have proved just as troublesome to overcome as in the Second World War. This despite the advent of the atomic bomb and other sophisticated weapons, but a pillbox with a good layer of earth covering its concrete could make an excellent fall-out shelter in the Third World War.

APPENDIX D

Bibliography of selected books

The Invasion Threat:
The Invasion of Britain Admiral Richmond, Methuen, 1941
Operation Sea Lion Ronald Wheatley, Oxford, 1958
Defence 1940:
The Defence of the United Kingdom Basil Collier, HMSO, 1960
The Second World War Vol 2 – Winston Churchill, Cassell, 1949
The Ironside Diaries 1937 to 1940 Field-Marshal Lord Ironside, Constable,
The Turn of the Tide Arthur Bryant, Collins, 1958
The Home Guard of Britain Charles Graves, Hutchinson, 1943
We Also Served – Home Guard in Cambridge Private, 1944
The Real Dad's Army Norman Longmate, Arrow, 1974
Invasion 1940 Peter Fleming, Rupert Hart-Davis, 1957
Britain's Home Guard John Brophy, Harrap, 1945
The Last Ditch David Lampe, Cassell, 1968
Also many Army and Home Guard histories which have chapters dealing with this period.
Books on Tactics:
New Ways of War Tom Wintringham, Penguin, 1940
The Home Guard Training Manual Murray, 1940
The Home Guard Fieldcraft Manual Murray, 1942
Advanced Training for the HG Hodder, 1941
Harrying the Hun Norman Demuth, Crowther,
Home Guard for Victory Hugh Slater, Gollancz, 1941
Also the official publications by the War Office.
The Home Front:
The Phoney War on the Home Front E. S. Turner, Michael Joseph, 1961

The People's War: Britain 1939–45 Angus Calder, Jonathan Cape, 1969
How We Lived Then Norman Longmate, Hutchinson, 1971
Keep Smiling Through Susan Briggs, Weidenfeld & Nicholson, 1975
The Countryside at War Grant & Maddern, Jupiter, 1975
War on the Line Bernard Darwin, Southern Railway, 1946
Ack Ack Sir Frederick Pile, Harrap, 1949
The German Invasion in Fiction:
The Invasion William Le Queux, Newnes, 1903
If Hitler Comes Douglas Brown and Christopher Serpell, Faber, 1940
Attack Alarm Hammond Innes, Collins, 1941
When the Bells Rang Anthony Armstrong & Bruce Graeme, Harrap, 1943
Sea Lion Richard Cox, Futura, 1974
England Under Hitler Comer Clarke, Ballantine, 1961
If Britain had Fallen Norman Longmate, Hutchinson,
The Home Guard in Fiction:
Home Guard Goings-on Basil Boothroyd, Allen & Unwin, 1941
Keep the Home Guard Turning Compton Mackenzie Chatto & Windus, 1943
From Dusk till Dawn A. G. Street, Harrap, 1943
Historical:
The Pillboxes of Flanders Col. E. G. L. Thurlow, British Legion, 1933

96

PILLBOXES: Index